S1

UNDERSTANDING THE DEAF/BLIND CHILD

D1471026

THE DEAF-BLIND MANUAL ALPHABET

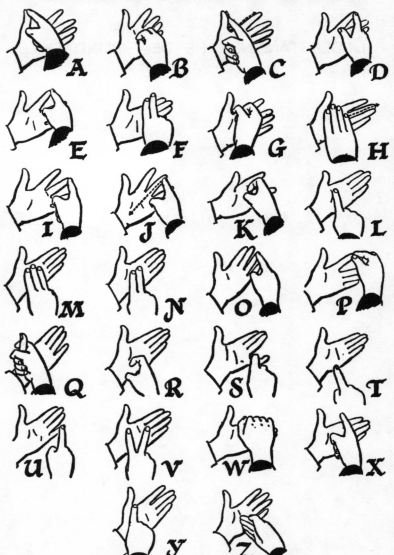

UNDERSTANDING THE DEAF/BLIND CHILD

Peggy Freeman M.B.E.

HEINEMANN HEALTH BOOKS
London

First published 1975

© Peggy Freeman 1975

ISBN 0 433 10905 X

"Heinemann Health Books" are published
by William Heinemann Medical Books Ltd

Photoset, printed and bound
in Great Britain by
REDWOOD BURN LIMITED
Trowbridge & Esher

CONTENTS

ACKNOWLEDGEMENTS

This book could not have been written without the help of many people, too many to name, and not least of all the children themselves including Bunty, who have been my inspiration.

It is a book for the parents whose courage in the face of tremendous difficulties has encouraged me to try to gather together the information they need to help them with their task and to organise it in such a way that they know where they are going and how to get there.

I also hope that teachers will find it useful when working with parents or with the very slow-learning deaf/blind child in school. To teachers in various disciplines I owe much and I would like to thank all those who provided me with programmes from which items are included in Chapter 11 Part 2, in particular my daughter Ann Jenkins, Miss J. Shields, Mrs. Hills, Mr. A. Best, Mr. J. Dale, Mrs. I. Hulse, & Miss M. Evans.

I should also like to express my gratitude to Miss E. M. Johnson and Dr. J. Reynell for their good advice in connection with the early chapters and to my husband for his never failing patience and support whilst I have been engaged on this task.

Finally, I should like to thank the National Deaf/Blind Child Rubella Association for their generous support given toward the promotion of this book.

Peggy Freeman
June, 1974

INTRODUCTION

A Personal Note

"It is easy to be wise after the event"—a well-worn phrase, but it describes the years that have passed since the day my deaf/blind daughter Bunty was born and today, when I sit down to write the first part of a book to help parents of similarly handicapped children. Ours is not a success story—very far from it. On my part it has been long years of learning what I *should* have done, and on Bunty's part, hard years of trying to respond to teaching that was either unsuitable, too advanced or given her when it was past the best time for that particular phase of learning.

As I had German measles (rubella) very early in pregnancy I knew my child might be born handicapped, but I was hardly prepared for sight, hearing and heart all to be affected—she looked so small and pale, and was so cold and motionless, that I think no-one expected her to survive the early weeks. I have been asked many times since how I felt when I knew Bunty was so severely handicapped, but there was so much to do with feeding, sleeping and general health problems, visits to this and that specialist, hospitalisation for eye operations, plus three lively older children to cope with, that I had little time to feel anything at all but tiredness and very often frustration.

At about 18 months we began to tackle the deafness with a hearing aid (an enormous thing tied to the side of the cot!) and regular visits to a clinic 2 hours away for guidance on the training. In those days I certainly did not understand the effect on the total development of a child when something is wrong with both the sight and the hearing—we worked away as if she was deaf praying that the sight she appeared to possess would prove sufficient for lipreading in time. Our main aim was to develop communication by speech, with the (quite crazy) idea that once we did teach her to speak, we would reason with her and by this means overcome the other problems. Of course we now realise that most of the time we spent "ba-ba"-ing into the mike in terms of lesson periods would have been far better spent teaching Bunty to feed herself, dress herself and all the other important self-care items which to this day still cause problems. With today's better understanding of the complex way in which children develop, we can get our priorities in better order and we can appreciate that no one thing comes first, but all the progress a child makes in one or several areas are necessary to progress in another or other directions.

If we ever looked into the future, and I think we only did in a hazy way, we thought in terms of how much we must help Bunty to make up for the hearing and sight loss—today we know the only sensible way to tackle the difficult task of bringing up any handicapped child is not to cry for the moon, but to see such a child (as any other) who has certain abilities—our task and that of all who along life's road will in turn share with us this task, is to see that our child makes the best possible use of these abilities, never mind about the things he doesn't possess, use those he has.

When Bunty was 6+ she went to a school for the deaf, but in 2 years she had outgrown the nursery class in size but was not advanced enough to move up a class. So she moved on to another school for the deaf into a small class of 4. Two year's later at 10 after an appeal to the Department of Education and Science against a decision of "ineducable", she went for 4 years to the Rudolf Steiner Camphill School in Aberdeen as a boarder—and these were happy years of slow progress for her, although we hated the long breaks from home. Once again at 15 this school also felt that her progress was too slow to warrant a place and, since it was so near to the end of her school days, we did not seek another school. Fortunately by this time experimental work with young children with the double handicap at Lea Hospital, Bromsgrove, was also extended to school-excluded and Bunty took her place there and, as I write, is still there, coming home to us every weekend.

However low Bunty's true potential may be, I am certain her inability to respond to educational methods tried so patiently with her by so many wonderful teachers, is related to the lack of home training in the very early years. We wanted so much to help her but there was no real body of information available. We shared experiences with other parents through the "Rubella Group" which we formed (now the National Asscn. for Deaf/Blind and Rubella Chn.) and I sought help from schools and other Associations for handicapped children in this country and abroad—we spread what we learned through the medium of the Group Newsletter and Progress Reports and gradually people became aware of this small group of children and set about helping them and their parents more specifically.

Whilst Bunty was at Camphill at the request of the Inner London Education Authority, I began to visit the homes of some of the London deaf/blind children to help their parents and then to teach 6 of them in a preschool unit. After 3 years I took the 3-year teacher training course since when I have had $2\frac{1}{2}$ years in charge of the Nursery Department of a school for children with specific learning difficulties and where I was also responsible for a remedial language group. At present I am in my second year as the educator member of a team assessing severely handicapped children aged 18 mos. to 5 years in a Centre attached to a Hospital. It is largely upon the experiences of the past 4 years that I have been able to write the chapters on the preschool deaf/blind child. Today there is undoubtedly recognition of the special educational needs of deaf/blind children and provision is slowly increasing and the stigma of "ineducability" a thing of the past. But to my mind there is still failure to reach parents early enough so that they can be taught to see how vital a part they can and must play before their child ever goes to school. Schooldays are only a very minute part of a life time and they are not the only time when a child is learning—he learns from the very first moment he draws breath and by the time a normal child goes to school the foundations for all his future learning, at school and elsewhere, are already laid. This book is intended to help lay these good foundations to learning for the deaf/blind child and to bring meaning into the world for him through whatever sight and hearing he does have. How succesful you are depends on your attitude to your child and your confidence in your own ability to help him—both of which stem from understanding his needs and knowing how to meet them. I hope in the following pages to help you realise some of the difficulties your child faces and to give you some ideas on what to do to develop his natural abilities as fully as possible.

PEGGY FREEMAN

CHAPTER 1
GETTING THINGS INTO PERSPECTIVE

You have a child with a sight and hearing handicap—it's a blow when you first learn that your baby is so severely handicapped. I know because it happened to me. It takes a lot of getting used to and if we are not careful we can waste precious time wondering why it should happen to us, to our child and how ever shall we cope. There is no answer to the first part of our questioning, but today we can begin to answer the last part. Deaf/blind children can be helped and more by their parents than any other person they will ever come into contact within all their childhood years.

The sooner we begin the better, but before we can begin, there are certain things we would do well to be aware of and try to understand. Suppose we aim to make a cake. We might have an idea of how to go about it and put in all the things we think we should, pop it in the oven, guessing the temperature and cooking time. It might turn out to be a super cake or it might equally well be uneatable. To be absolutely certain of a good cake we must know the right ingredients, how much of each, when to add them—what to substitute if an ingredient is not available, whether to cook slowly or quickly, and so on. This may be an odd parallel to draw between a cake and bringing up a handicapped child—but it is also true that if we aim to make the best possible job of the latter, we need to know what we aim for, how the child develops (the ingredients), the order in which development takes place (the mixing) and whether we should go slowly or push him along to catch up. It may take extra time and trouble to consult the cookery book, but when you taste the result it was worth it—so too it is well worth getting the right "recipe" for helping your child firmly in your mind and sticking to it. You can make another cake if at first you fail, but you do not have a second chance to bring up a handicapped child if you fail to make a good start.

Aim
We must be realistic—expecting a miracle cure just is not on. Even if it were possible to put things right at some time, even during the very early years, being without full sight and hearing at the beginning or at any time in a child's life is bound to affect every aspect of his

1

development and colour the adult he will be. Nevertheless a miracle does happen when day by day you help him use his abilities to the full and you see him moving forward. How far forward he goes is less important than that he should ultimately have gone far enough to be able to lead a life that is happy and satisfying for *him*. This we keep in mind for the future—our everyday aims will be more concrete.

Child Development

Given a loving family background and lots to do, most children grow up without us being aware of what is happening to them, but it is generally accepted that all children, in growing up, must show development in the following areas:

Sensory	—seeing, hearing, touching, smelling and tasting.
Motor	—becoming active in an increasingly skilful way.
Emotional	—loving, hating, etc.
Social	—behaving in the same way as others.
Communication	—speaking, signing, writing, reading.

A handicapped child may develop normally in some areas and be slow in others—we need to know something about the areas so that we recognise his strong points in order not to hold him back in them and to make use of them to help him in his weak areas.

Sequence and Timing

We all know that children develop their skills in a certain order—we would not, for instance, expect a child to run before he could walk. Thanks for years of careful child study child specialists have been able to provide us with a description of the step by step sequence of development which is common to *all* children and these steps are *our* day-to-day goals. The deaf/blind child will walk before he runs, but he is going to take longer to learn to walk and much longer than the average child to learn to get from walking to running. He is unlikely to get as far along the sequence as a child who sees and hears properly, but he must still follow the same sequence at his own pace ... he will probably never read Shakespeare, but reading Shakespeare is not essential to a happy and satisfying life.

Your Attitude

As you begin to work with your child you will find it less difficult than you expected. It gradually becomes habit to handle and help him in the appropriate way and you find you are less concerned with trying to overcome the handicaps than to reach the normal milestones despite the handicaps. Don't make comparisons of age with other normal or handicapped children—your child is unique—so long as he is on the way to achieving the next small step forward, you can sing his praises.

Often children seem to reach some stage and stick there for rather long—we need to recognise this also so that we can try a different line of approach rather than push harder, possibly too hard.

No parent is naturally equipped to bring up a handicapped child —most of us have to learn quite a lot by trial and error and we must never be afraid to seek out help and accept it when offered.

The Handicaps

A child who has absolutely no sight and no hearing is rare—most children termed deaf/blind have some sight and hearing and the term is used if, together, these handicaps make it impossible for him to be educated in a school for the blind or a school for the deaf. The same kind of early help is needed whenever there is some degree of hearing loss and sight loss—it is by the response to the early help that specialists are helped to determine the extent of the handicaps and assess the best kind of school.

There are children born with the double handicap whose mothers have not had german measles in pregnancy, but this is the most frequent cause. Here deafness is usually partial, the eyes (or one eye only) are affected by cataracts or retinal damage, the former responding to treatment. The heart is often affected and usually this is a "patent ductus" which if necessary can be corrected by operation. We must accept the fact that a virus which has damaged these vital parts of the baby before he is born may also have harmed parts of his brain. Whilst this may make it harder for him to learn, it does not mean that he cannot learn at all. In such cases we shall have to have a bit more patience, be a bit more ingenious in the way we help him and not expect him to go quite so far.

Up to this point I have assumed that the double handicap is certain—the rubella sight defect can be seen at birth or within a few days, it is not so easy to be certain that your baby is deaf at this early age. If there is a history of rubella in the pregnancy, deafness can be suspected—your child is "at risk"—and to guard against losing valuable time waiting for a definite diagnosis, training for the double handicap can be begun. If after a while your child responds to what he is hearing and makes the normal beginnings to understanding what you say to him, and to speaking, then you will be advised to put aside the methods for the double handicap and concentrate on those for a child with the sight difficulty only. Similarly if by operation your child's sight improves and he gives evidence of seeing and understanding what he sees, then also you will leave aside training geared to the combined defect and treat him as a deaf child. In either case no harm will have been done by the overall stimulation designed for the very young deaf /blind baby.

CHAPTER 2
THE FIRST WEEKS

Communication—The need for "clues" as part of handling

Although for the reasons I have already mentioned you are unlikely to have such a book as this immediately after the birth of your handicapped baby, the first 'work' with him does in fact begin when you hold him in your arms forgetting for a moment the natural anxieties about the future, and love him just because he is a baby.

Newborn babies need love, warmth, food and sleep—*all* of them. To begin with the only contact they have with the world around them is during the routines we use when we are feeding, undressing, bathing, dressing or changing nappies. Although the sight and hearing are not fully developed at birth, what he dimly sees and hears provides the baby with his first clues. Because these clues keep occurring regularly, the baby comes to recognise them, to link them with what is happening to him and then to anticipate them—he is "learning"—e.g., he makes sucking actions just before he is fed.

The deaf/blind baby cannot receive his clues this way and unless we provide a substitute system through touch and smell, he will miss out on this early learning which is absolutely necessary as the foundation for future learning. For instance your baby is nice and warm and cosy in his cot and he sees and hears nothing to warn him that you have come to the cot and are about to pick him up say to give him a bath —out of the blue a pair of hands take him up in the air, put him down again in a place that is not his cosy cot, his clothes are taken off, he is lifted again and put in yet another strange environment—imagine this had happened to you and then on top of it all a wet soapy hand you had not seen coming slides over your body—quite enough to upset you (and your appetite) for the rest of the day! Even when you got used to the idea that this would happen frequently, you would still be likely to feel fear. Our first aim then is to learn to handle the deaf/blind baby in this special "clue giving" way—it becomes habit after a time and it's a good habit to acquire early because deaf/blind children always need extra clues. Here are some suggestions for use when handling to give you an idea of what I mean. At all times just before you go to pick up your baby from the cot or pram, lay your hand very gently on him and leave it there for a few seconds—this is to become the signal that

4

something is going to happen to him. If he is in a cot with a drop side, give him this signal before you let the side down and do let it down gently. Lift him slowly and firmly from the cot and make the place in your lap as cosy as the bed he has just left. Take your time undressing or changing him—baby clothes that slip on and off easily without him having to be moved about too much help to make it easy for you both. When it is bathtime have the room warm and the towel warmed. Try to have the bath the same height as your lap so that baby does not have the feeling of a drop as he goes into it. Your warning signal for this part of the routine could be just to dabble baby's hand in the warm water before actually immersing his body. Be very careful about the heat of the bath—if your baby has a heart defect his feet and hands may be extra cold and what seems to you to be a suitable temperature for his body may actually feel burning to his toes and fingers. An experience of this kind can make bathing something to be feared for a very long time which is a pity, because deaf/blind children get a lot of pleasure from the feel of water as well as useful limb movement. If your baby's feet and hands feel cold before the bath, warm them gently until they are the same temperature as the rest of his body, *do not* make the water cooler. Another useful clue to bathtime is the soap —one with a strong pleasant smell which you can hold within smelling distance just before you begin to use it. The bath is over—warn him he is coming out by touching his face with the towel. When he is dressed (clues for this come later) fed and ready to go back to cot or pram, put him in and give him a clue that you are going to leave him —this must be quite different from the picking up one and like all signs only ever used for the particular part of the routine for which it has been designed—in this instance a suitable sign might be a movement of your hand across his forehead as if you were smoothing back his hair.

Social and Emotional—Feeding

Feeding problems (for which these children are well known) often begin at birth although it is more usual for them to become really obvious by weaning time. You may find that your baby takes a long time to take his feed—this can be very wearing and frustrating to you, particularly if your baby is breastfed. What you have to realise is that feeding is more than just putting food into the baby so that he will grow in size and thrive—it is a time of close contact with mother which is important to the emotional development. You both need to be comfortable, relaxed and to enjoy it—if *you* are worried about poor feeding or anxious to get it over and done with because there are other urgent things to do, your child will sense your tenseness and will be upset by it. Whatever else you hurry over, go out of your way to organise your day so that feeding times are unhurried and peaceful—if baby is a slow feeder you have to accept this fact as one which, for the time being, you cannot alter.

Feeding problems are worrying to us, but if we pass on our anxiety to the child we are adding to his difficulties rather than lessening them. Don't worry too much if your baby takes less food than expected—we all vary in the amount and kind of food we take and in the amount we need to take. These babies seem able to thrive on less than the average child and so long as what is taken is enjoyed, it doesn't seem to make much difference to the size and weight to which he finally grows. A child with a heart defect will feed more slowly because feeding and digesting what he has taken requires considerable effort and he will tend to tire more quickly. Be guided by your doctor as to how often to feed, but if you find your baby shows a preference for a particular rhythm (say a smaller feed at certain times) and is more contented this way, meet his needs. It is more important that feeding is a happy time than that you insist that it takes place at regular times or insist on him taking the amount that might be right for the average child.

Our overall intentions in what we are doing is to make life enjoyable and meaningful for the baby—if he likes what is happening right from the beginning, he is likely to go on enjoying life, but if he finds it frightening, he may let his fears prevent him ever learning that it can be enjoyable. Because the substitute clues are not so effective as those from seeing and hearing, our baby will take longer to learn them —stick to the routine you set and do not change until you are sure he has learned to anticipate it, and only then introduce something different which will include the old clue plus the new.

Not only must baby enjoy life, but we must enjoy him. Try not to think too far ahead, he is a baby like any other and needs to be enjoyed as such. He will need more and more of your time as he gets older, so get out and enjoy yourself in these early months whilst he can be safely left with others—this is good for you and what is good for you, is also good for your baby.

6

CHAPTER 3
UP TO SITTING UP

Communication
Once your baby begins to be awake for longer periods and becomes more active, you need to be thinking how you can stimulate him to use the sight and hearing he has, and how you can encourage him to practice movements that will strengthen the muscles needed to reach the first milestone along the road to sitting alone—that is head control. Of course you must continue to use and *add to* the clues. For your own reference (and that of others who may now handle your baby more often) keep a note of these clues and the context in which they are used. Only by using the same one to convey the same meaning time and time again will it come to be recognised and represent the beginning of communication from you to your baby. Keep a pad and pencil on a hook on the wall in the room in which you handle baby most and get into the babit of jotting such things down.

Sensory
(a) Sight
So far we have been mainly concerned with what we do *to* baby—by now he should be beginning to do things himself—ordinarily he would be looking and listening, moving about, learning about what is around him and what is going on, all the time getting better at and recognising more of it. Our deaf/blind baby cannot be looking and learning to the same extent. If he is a "rubella" baby, there is a good chance he may have some useful sight when the cataracts have been needled, but to begin with, it might be said he is looking at the world through greaseproof paper. Light getting through this to the retina helps to keep the eye developing and seeing things as differences in light and darkness can give the child a limited amount of information. Some of the pleasure the normal baby experiences when he begins to recognise what he sees is felt by the deaf/blind baby through this light perception as it is called. You will notice him looking at the electric light in the room, in the direction of the window or at a torch light if you wave this about.
The natural position for the very young baby awake in his pram or cot is with his arm and hand between his head and the light. A seeing baby watches his hand in this position and learns to focus his two eyes as a

7

result—at first his hand moves aimlessly, then when he can focus, he learns to move it deliberately in order to see it move. Our baby should be aware of the changing pattern of light as he moves his arm and whilst we cannot help him learn to focus until the cataracts have been needled, we can encourage the variety of movement in the arms and hands. Create a light and darkness situation—a lamp on the level at the side of the pram or cot, sunlight through the window, sunshine through the moving leaves and branches of a tree. Remember that if we only place the pram or cot one way, he will learn to use only one arm and hand and he will not be encouraged to move his head to both sides which is part of the development of control of head. Put him in as many different positions as possible in relation to the direction of the light that attracts him, putting the light above, to either side, in front of and behind him. The seeing baby would soon now be noticing mummy moving about and coming to him—can you think of ways in which you, using light, to encourage your baby to watch you and move to follow you with his eyes?

(b) Hearing—Listening

Before we consider the next stage in this area it is helpful to under-stand how children progress from just listening, as the baby does, to being able to understand what you say to him and to be able to talk to you so that you know what he means, by the time he is about 3. What baby first hears is probably just one big jumble of sounds. Gradually he becomes aware that some of them happen again and again in associ-ation with something pleasurable (mother's voice, the bells on his pram toy) or with something unpleasant (a door that bangs). It is a long time before a child has heard these often enough to pick them out in this way, longer still to connect them with the actual source.

A hearing child hears mother's voice wherever she is in the room and he hears clearly all the words she says, and hears them over and over again, day in, day out. A child with only partial hearing needs to be close to his mother to hear her voice—even with a hearing aid maybe no more than a few feet away—what he hears may lack clarity or he may miss part of words and for this reason if for no other may be less motivated to listen. Our job at this stage is to encourage baby to listen and this means bringing sounds close to him and making these mean-ingful and interesting. Talk to him just as you would a hearing baby with your lips close to his ear to give him the best chance of hearing. He gets extra clues from the puffs of air that come from your mouth as you speak and above all he is made aware that it is you, his mother, making the sounds he hears or feels.

Do not raise your voice because this distorts speech sounds—speak in your normal voice. If baby doesn't seem to like this closeness to begin with, speak softly or sing so that you can also move rhythmically and

8

gain his interest this way. If your baby has been given a hearing aid, use it the same way, holding the mike in your hand about 6 inches from your lips and see that somehow the breath and vibration clues also reach baby otherwise the sound will have no source.

Emotional

Listening to her voice is part of baby's recognition of his mother, full recognition of her is one of the first positive signs we have from him. First mother builds up a knowledge of herself for the normal and the deaf/blind baby through the way she does things to him, but the realisation of mother as a person separate from the rest of things comes to a seeing baby through a special interaction which goes on between mother and child. For example baby smiles at mother because she smiles at him, his smile makes mother smile back and this gives them both a happy feeling—it happens again and again as mummy is nursing him, attending to him or just passing by his pram. This is something very important to the development of a child's emotional stability and something our baby misses and which we can make up for only in part. Instead of smiling at him we shall have to fondle him physically more often than we might a seeing child, play more tickling games—this can be while he is lying in his pram or in your arms—if the latter, do a little before you pick him up so that he comes to know he is going to be picked up for a game.

In addition we can give him something to know us by through his touching us—place his hand on your cheek when you pick him up and see that no-one else uses this signal. Or you can wear a particular brooch which he can touch, or to use his sense of smell you can wear a strong perfume which he can come to associate with you alone. Daddy might well come to be recognised by the smell of tobacco or a bristly chin! The important thing is that mummy begins to be recognised for herself—he has to make a relationship with you and trust you before he can make relationships with other people and trust them to help him. Your arms must become a safe place from which to "view" the world and your hands his first guide to finding out what it is made of. You can now set aside a short period several times a day when you nurse your baby. Often deaf/blind children seem to prefer lying in their pram or cot and show signs of distress if nursed for other than handling routines. It is fatal to give in to him and leave him on his own on the pretext that you are keeping him happy—it may be an easy way out for you, but in reality it is the worst possible thing for him. If your baby is like this, find something he likes doing and let him do it on your lap—it's even worth denying him any other opportunity to do it except on your lap—do it regularly at the beginning of the nursing period so that he comes to recognise the activity and associate it with you. Remember that a child learns to love only by being loved, by being

9

close to you and doing things he enjoys with you.

Widening the scope of experience

Gradually now we can widen the range of experiences our baby has in relation to his age and to the stage he has reached in the developmental sequence. Many of these experiences still and always will occur within the daily routines and the rest we shall have deliberately to put before him in such a way that they enable him to build up his learning about the world around him and is motivated to learn more.

New routines will become necessary and we shall have to make some changes in the old ones. Once you have decided the change is necessary, set about making it in gradual stages and once embarked *do not go back to the old one*. A change in routine to the baby is in fact making an alteration in something you have been at great pains to get him used to and to recognise, so he may object, but do not weaken.

Social and Emotional
(a) Feeding

This is a routine which changes now and is a good example of what I mean. We are all apt to worry if we think a child is not getting what we consider is enough nourishment—a baby who doesn't much care for the strange feel of solids in his mouth may well refuse to swallow them and scream for his smooth milk. If we give in and let him have his milk so that he does not miss a feed, he will know how to get his milk next time and every time after that. In this respect handicapped children are no different from any other and because they cannot see others enjoying this strange food and hear Mummy say how nice it is, they can be most persistent in their refusal. Unless there is some physical reason why your child cannot swallow solids, he should be able to begin to be weaned at the same age as all children, but we can help him make the change gradually.

Initially begin giving the ordinary milk on a spoon at one feed a day —he may take all this feed this way or only a few spoonfuls, but do not give him anything else at this feed which is probably preferably the mid-day one. If the quantity he takes is small, then make the *next* meal slightly bigger than usual or give it a little earlier. When baby is used to taking milk from the spoon at this feed each day, thicken it, almost imperceptibly, with a fine cereal. If the same pattern of behaviour as with the first milk from a spoon appears, use the same method to overcome it—i.e., adjust the next feed. "Rubella" children very often find the change a hard one to make and it does seem to be related to consistency (thickness) rather than dislike of a flavour. Begin very very slowly rather than offering a spoonful of normally mixed cereal at the start to see if he can take it—such an experience can frighten him off ever trying again for months and even years. When you feel he accepts

10

the new food and takes sufficient for the feed, add a little more cereal and continue this procedure until he reaches the normal consistency. If a certain thickness is strongly rejected, go back to the previous thickness—never go back to normal milk for this feed once cereal has been introduced. Very finely mashed potatoes or the baby tins of chicken broth, neither of them very strong flavours, can be used as well as the cereal. It is better to get the consistency accepted, before we introduce new stronger flavours. When you do try new flavours make sure the consistency is the same as that which he accepts happily.

The upsetting of one meal a day is not going to affect a child's health as much as if, by trying to force down a whole meal of thickened food, you make feeding a time of tears and stress. It is true that a baby might come to recognise this feed and, knowing other feeds will follow, refuse to have any at all. He does need to be hungry to take something he doesn't like yet and you could reduce the quanity of the previous feed slightly to ensure this. At any rate every day at this feed he should be offered the cereal—patience, understanding and persistence on your part should win the day.

Change from breast feeding or bottle to use of the cup for liquids should also be made about now, but is also often a problem. If the introduction of solids is difficult it might be wisest to delay the introduction of a cup until your baby has got used at least to having solids as part of his regular diet and accepts small quantities. Apart from the various commercial baby feeding cups which can be useful as intermediary steps, the best way is, as with the solids, to introduce it slowly. First only a touch of the cup to baby's lips—possibly with a spot of milk or honey on the rim—to get him used to the feel of it at his mouth.

When you begin with the actual drink only put a few spoonfuls in—he may at first not know how to hold the milk in his mouth by cupping his bottom lip round the cup and will dribble copiously if there is too much in the cup. Once he has regular experience he will learn these things —give him milk from a cup only at one meal a day, the same meal each day and if possible the one when he appears to be most thirsty. Don't delay too long before starting to use a cup—a child who has sucked from a bottle too long past the normal period for sucking, can end up sucking all his food as well instead of chewing it—since the muscles used for chewing are also important for speech, this can have a bearing on a child's future ability to speak.

Solids such as rusks, toast, crusts, etc., should be introduced now by just touching them to baby's lips and holding his fingers round them for a few seconds (for smell, the feel of them and the feel of them at the mouth, possibly taste too). It is best to do this just before the tea-time feed—we are not concerned with their nourishment value—just

11

to make them familiar to him—if he likes them right away and begins to eat them, so much the better.

The most important points about feeding are:

It must never become a stress situation.

Introduce changes very gradually.

Never go back once a change has been begun.

Be patient and persistent—better to take solids and use a cup well as late as 3 years than still be on a bottle only at 4 years.

(b) Toilet Training

This is a new routine which we can begin to introduce at this stage in terms of helping baby to become familiar with the feel of the pottie and the routines involved, rather than being concerned with getting him trained. Lots of normal children object initially to toilet training and success first depends on a child's physical ability, i.e., the development of the muscles and the control of these necessary to perform . . . no training system can succeed before the child is physically ready, and there is often delay in this area of development, particularly with "rubella" children. Toilet training techniques will be included in each of the sections of this book, here we are merely concerned with the first steps. At bathtime before putting on the fresh nappy, sit baby on the pottie which has been warmed and is on your lap between your knees, cuddle him so he feels secure. Once this is accepted, you can begin doing it at some other changing times and then just briefly at every nappy change. If we can get our baby used to the feel of sitting on the pottie half the battle is won—when he is able to use it, he will.

(c) Breaks in routine

Unfortunately these can occur all too often in the first 2 years for eye ops, diagnostic observation or hospital checkups. If you can accompany your child and maintain as much as possible of a recognised routine, so much the better, but even so some upset can be expected when the child returns. Right away go back to the handling routines which were well established before he went away—do not try something new, he needs to get back the security that familiar things bring (even if he has forgotten some of them he will soon be reminded) and he needs to sense your confidence which will come of doing something you know he has already been able to manage. If feeding has reverted and it often does, use the same gradual procedures to get back to where you were, they shouldn't take so long to go through.

Motor Development

Any baby should be naturally active himself at this stage, kicking vigorously in his pram and bath and he should be getting used to being moved about by others in lots of different positions. Our baby may feel a little unsafe in any position other than on his back—if he does cling to the one position we need to get him used to being in different ones with and through us. We can hold him in lots of different ways—in our arms, on our laps, when we are standing up, sitting down, lying down —going from one position to another whilst he is in our arms, on our laps, etc. As an example—the baby who isn't too keen on lying on his tummy—one of the important positions from which to look around since it encourages head control—hold him up to one's shoulder, lean back slowly until you are lying down with the child on you on his tummy—get him used to this position, play with him in it, then using a bright light (window or torch) encourage him to watch it moving from side to side by turning his head. Gradually get him used to a few seconds on his own tummy on the bed and cushion on the floor. Make sure you use this position during bathing and nappy changing routine.

Progressing from the stage of lying on his back to sitting up alone is a difficult one for the deaf/blind baby. In some cases unless we help him, his preference for the lying position becomes so strong that he will resist all attempts to help him and become withdrawn. Like toiletting, a child must be ready physically before he can achieve sitting up, but we can encourage him to make the right kind of preparatory movements. The following will give you a rough idea of the sequence through which a baby has to go on the way to this milestone:

1. Lifts chin and face off pillow when on tummy.
2. Lifts head off pillow when on back.
3. If pulled to sitting position head lags slightly.
4. If pulled to sitting position supports head when held still.
5. Held sitting—no head wobble.
6. When pulled to sitting he anticipates by lifting head.
7. Sits supporting himself on hands.
8. Sits momentarily without support.

Interest in what he sees usually provides a baby with much of the incentive to motor development at this stage—he raises his head to look around, he rolls from tummy to back and from back to tummy and likes the different view of the world he gets, he watches moving things and discovers that if he moves they appear to move—movement helps him to learn about what he sees and seeing encourages movement. He moves to see where sounds come from, to see what he has touched or what has touched him. It is not surprising that this is where a deaf/blind baby begins to lag behind or why just giving him sitting up experience isn't enough to get him from this stage to the next. Sitting up has to be pleasant and interesting—it must provide him with something he doesn't get in any other position so that he comes to

13

want to sit up of his own accord. We may have to help him get used to the sitting up position to begin with and once again we must do it gradually as follows:

First. In the pram or cot during the day when awake.
Using a folded nappy (or something of similar thickness) put it under his normal pillow. When he seems used to this put another folded nappy under as well—and so on until he is resting back in such a way that he can no longer look up at the ceiling, but not so that his head falls forward. It may be necessary to devise a way of keeping him from slipping down to the lying position (a backrest with straps) also pillows to prevent slipping sideways.

Second. Nursing.
We will often already have had our baby sitting supported on our lap, now we want to do this more often particularly with his back against us and his legs over our knees—this is a position he will frequently occupy in the future when we are teaching him about things through feeling them with our help. Also now it is a good thing to play with him sitting in the opposite direction playing seesaw games, our hands supporting his head (if necessary) and his back. Using these two positions each for a specific purposese gives baby a clue to what is going to happen.
Not only do we want to get baby used to this position, but we also want him to learn to use his residual sight and hearing in this position. Sitting up brings a wider range of objects within his reach. All the normal pram toys can be enjoyed by our baby although he will probably prefer hard ones—the string of balls which stretch across the pram will provide a firm definite shape to hold. Although in the movements he will make naturally with his arms and hands he will bump into these toys, he may prefer waving his hands in front of his eyes to feeling and exploring the toys. The hand waving is such a source of pleasure to the rubella child that there is a real danger that this activity may continue too long outliving its developmental function and preventing the baby using his hands to explore and learn with them. If we find this, we must frequently put one of his hands on to the toy, then the other, then hold both gently round one of the balls or whatever it is. Now you can begin to get into another habit that is important to all future work with your baby. *Whenever you are guiding your baby's hands to help him learn with them stand behind him and put your hands over his*. This way whatever movements you make him do will be in the correct direction and not from a false angle as might happen if you guide his action from the front or the side.
If your baby is lucky enough to have colour perception this helps to make him interested in toys but generally speaking it is *familiarity* which first creates interest—the seeing baby is attracted by some-

14

thing new, the deaf/blind baby tends to be afraid of the new which mostly comes to him as an unfamiliar touch and our job is to bring the new to him through us. We must begin putting things into our baby's hands at the same stage as the seeing child would handle them for himself, otherwise it is possible for a complete aversion to holding anything to build up and so deprive baby of his main source of learning.

In addition to baby toys we can devise playthings which we can put into baby's hands and which he is likely to want to hold on to because they provide a reflective light pattern—a shiny tin lid, a piece of cardboard or any other material which has or can have a hole in the middle. We must guard against baby playing only with these and they might well provide the something for him to hold when he is on your lap (as mentioned previously). Hold the "toy" in your left hand with your right hand over baby's right hand, put this hand on the toy—change the position in which you hold it—it can be down in your lap, up in the air, over to the right or left, so that with your help he is reaching for the toy and finding it in various positions. Then do it with the other hand and finally put the toy on the table or in your lap and taking both baby's hands in yours, put them round the toy and hold it.

It is also time to begin putting your baby's hands on the things you use in the daily routines—i.e., the feeding bottle, the spoon, cup, dish; on the towel, the soap, the hairbrush (all very distinct sensations to touch). Introduce these things gradually—otherwise he will get confused if there are too many at once and if they are similar. Do not expect recognition to come quickly—if you make a note of when you introduced a new thing, another on the date you think he showed anticipation or recognition and then again note the date when you are absolutely certain it meant something to him, you will find the time between the dates becoming less and this is a sign that your system is working.

Summary

This has been rather a longwinded chapter, but a lot of explanation has been necessary. I hope by now you are beginning to "catch on" to the underlying basics—perhaps we might briefly recap:
We must begin:

(a) To start building up a sign system related to regular daily routines to help our baby understand what is going on.

(b) To ensure that being with mummy is enjoyable so that he is beginning to make a relationship with her.

(c) To stimulate him to move about because he needs to move to learn.

15

(d) To encourage him to use the residual sight and hearing.
(e) To widen his experiences through changing old and bringing in new routines.
(f) To gradually change from lying to sitting up.
(g) To use his hands.
(h) To increase the variety of his activities.

CHAPTER 4

FROM SITTING UP TO STANDING ALONE

First I must stress again that although the advice I have given assumes a fairly regular development in all areas, this may not be the case and delay in an area will become more apparent from now on. I have given an area reference so that if you find you have romped through any particular part of a chapter, you can look up the appropriate section in the next and start on the suggestions made there. For example getting on to solids may take a long time, but this is no reason to delay moving on to feeding with the child in a high-chair if the child is physically ready for this (can sit up comfortably). It is more than likely that sitting in the high-chair will improve his anticipation of feeding and help him accept the different foods.

From now on we shall be starting to introduce what we will call "communication signs" in addition to substitute clues. As baby grows up the daily routines change and many of the substitute clues drop out and others more suitable are used for a while and then these drop out to be replaced by others. Communication signs, however, are those signs which remain and do not change and later are also used by the child to the adult. For example, to show your child you are pleased with him or he is right in what he is doing, give him a pat on the head.

Motor—New Activities

Once the muscles that hold baby in the sitting position are strong enough he will be able to balance sitting alone for a few minutes without falling over. Next he has to learn to hold this position as long as he wishes and to move about as much as he wants to in this position. Babies practice this as they reach for and twist round to get things they see and hear, so our baby will need to be encouraged also to use his residual sight and hearing for the same purpose.

By now we should have a good idea where and at what distance we think our baby sees things best—it may be only 6 inches in front of him or several feet, one eye may be used more than the other, he may spot it more quickly if the object is moved about a bit. Hold a bright reflective toy in that position and let him reach for it and touch it there before you move it out of his sight range. Do this a few times (if baby doesn't reach for it of his own accord, two adults can make a game of

17

this, one having the toy, the other, the child in her lap, guiding his hand) then when his hand is just about to touch the toy, move it away just enough to tempt him to reach and make a slight balance adjustment. Continue the game—and it must be a *game* which by your laughter and praise you make him also feel the enjoyment—making him reach to find it in different positions and further in distance. Similarly tempt him to to look round for a sound he recognises and to reach for the object making this.

Give him lots of variety in sitting experience—on the floor, on a chair (all sorts of chairs) settee, bed, high up, low down, soft and hard seats, in this room, in that room, indoors, outdoors, in a car, etc., moving seats—indoor swing, rocking chairs, walkie pens, carrying sling, pushchair (an excellent special pushchair called a "Baby Buggy" which folds to almost nothing, takes up little room when open and is designed to keep the child in the sitting position is to be recommended so long as he doesn't come to live in it) and do not leave him in any one more than about 20 minutes at a time.

Whilst you have been holding your baby, romping with him, you will often have had him in the standing position—now we are en route to standing alone, he will enjoy this more often and will begin to try bearing his own weight and bouncing up and down on his feet, both pre-standing exercises which you can encourage him to do. Also encourage him to roll over from his back to his tummy and then from tummy to back, to lift his chest off the floor and take his weight on his arms, not as an exercise, but as fun and games.

Crawling comes about now, although some may well make the first move from one place to another by shuffling on their backs or on their bottoms. Babies tend to crawl backwards before forwards and it may help your baby to put him where he can push his hands or his legs against something hard to help give him the feel of movement back and forth. If he is attracted by light, put this to good use. Using a torch shine its beam on the floor just in front of him as he lies on his tummy, move it away a little and encourage him to try to put his hands on it and to move to reach it. If your baby already has learned to wriggle to get himself into the sunlight you can deliberately move him out of it, put him on his tummy and taking him through the motions help him crawl back to it (use a lamp on a dull day). Do this a few times every day until you feel baby trying to make some of the necessary crawling movements for himself after which you gradually lessen the amount of help you give him until he manages by himself. Don't let him roll over halfway and use his own method of locomotion for the rest of the way otherwise you have defeated the object of the exercise. The distance he has to crawl must be short to begin with and as he gets more skilful, you can increase it. If baby has quite a bit of useful sight a bright toy on the floor which he is allowed to play with once he has crawled to get it, may be sufficient to encourage crawling.

The following are some of the stages we can expect baby to reach during this period:

Stands holding on to something, unable to get back to sitting position by himself.

Standing with support can lower himself to sitting on floor.

Walks with two hands held.

Stands alone momentarily.

Once baby stands happily with you supporting him, you can begin pre-walking practice. With his back leaning against you, his hands held in yours, put his feet on top of yours and go through the motions of walking (very tiny steps) forwards, backwards, sideways—instead of him learning how to walk by watching others as the seeing baby does, you are giving him the feeling of what walking is like. When you progress to trying him walking himself, with both hands held, he will need extra clues about balance which comes through changing his weight from one foot to the other (which is what we all do when we walk). It is best if two people help him here—daddy holds his hand one side, mummy the other, first one pulls him gently to their side until, because you are making him change his weight the foot on the other side leaves the ground, then the other does the same on the other side—a kind of rocking movement from side to side which can be just on the one spot to begin with and then gradually giving a slight forward bias so that the foot coming off the floor returns to the ground a bit further forward and is a step in the right direction.

He is also about ready to learn to get by himself from lying down to sitting up and from sitting to lying. We can give him practice by sitting with him on the floor, his legs either side of us so that when he lies down he is along the length of our legs. Holding his two hands we can pull him from this lying position to sitting and then let him gently back—play seesaw, singing to give a steady rhythm to the movement, he will enjoy this. When he is used to the exercise he will probably indicate he wants to go on playing by giving a tug at your hands to pull him up—you give him less and less help returning his tug to show he has to try a little for himself until he comes up and down for himself. Also, if we sit on the floor with him, draw up our knees and sit him up on them, we can let him down gently and give him the experience of going downwards as part of the preparation for getting from standing back to sitting.

Try to see that all these activities come somewhere in your play with him each day—there should be no pressure to do them, only encouragement gently, but *regularly*. You will begin to notice some of the movements being practiced when he is playing by himself. If you feel baby is lagging behind in motor development, do discuss this with your doctor—he may recommend physiotherapy.

Social
(a) Feeding
The variety of taste and texture of the food taken should be on the increase now. Beware of letting your child get "stuck" on one particular flavour for too long—all children tend to develop special likes and dislikes, but there are so many ways of persuading normal children to try new things that are denied to deaf/blind children. When you do feel this happening, try offering something else at the feed the baby would have had the preferred food, and even if he refuses it do not give the one he likes at all for this feed—make up with a drink of milk. Or you can try giving him alternate spoons of the one he likes and the one he dislikes. These are just two suggestions—you will probably hit on other solutions which will get you over this. Always bear in mind that feeding is not only necessary for nourishment, but is also essentially a "social" area in which we want our child to learn to behave as near as possible to others, and this includes the ability to enjoy variety in food.

He should now be fed in a high chair because this frees you to provide him with more clues to the feeding experience as well as being a step forward. As in most situations throughout the early years you can never go far wrong if you say to yourself—what would a seeing /hearing child get out of this routine and then set about finding out how to give the deaf/blind child the same sort of information in a different form. Say you are going to give baby a bowl (plastic) of cereal off a spoon. The normal baby watches you get the cereal packet and hears the sound of it shaking inside; he sees you tip it into the bowl, pour over the milk, hears the spoon clatter round the bowl as you mix it, he gets a whiff of the smell, sees you bringing it towards him, he knows it is for him and begins to jig about with anticipation, making eating movements; when he sees the spoon coming towards his mouth, he opens it ready, swallows the food and seeing your look of approval, opens it again for the next; when it is finished you show him it is empty and tell him what a good boy he was to eat it all. If you do nothing but stuff the cereal into the deaf/blind baby and then go away and wash up the bowl, what a desolate experience his has been! Instead you could hold him in your arms when you got the cereal and let him feel it (he would have learned something of the feel of cardboard and of the shape of the box) shaken it close to his ear with his hand on it so that he could feel it moving up and down inside. Then he could have felt the jug of warm milk and smelled it, and put his hand on and in the dish and let him hold the spoon. Once you have alerted him to the feed in this way, you can put him in the highchair, mix the cereal noisily and close enough for him to hear the spoon against the dish, when ready let him feel the dish and then the food in it with his finger.

20

Then holding it at the distance you feel he sees best, (and holding it there until he *has* seen it,) offer him the first spoonful, giving him time to open his mouth in anticipation—from now on hold the full spoon within his sight range, the bowl can be put down. If the sight is very poor, then just touch his lips with the spoon, moving away a little to give him time to open his mouth in anticipation. When it is all gone (or if he has left some but had enough, empty it without him knowing) let him feel the emptiness and chat away to him about what a good boy he is, never forgetting the pat on the head for approval. When the preparation of the feed is not so easy or it has been preprepared, let the child have a smell or touch it before you put him in the chair. Have him sitting in the kitchen when you are preparing meals so he can hear the clatter of pans and smell the foods you are cooking.

Now also is the time to lay the foundation for our next communication sign which will be the drinking sign. At this stage it is a matter of holding baby's hand round the bottle or cup from which he is drinking (remember you stand behind his chair). The hand in this position moved up and down to the mouth is the sign we will ultimately expect your child to make to tell you he is thirsty or which you will make to him to inform him you are getting him a drink or to ask him if he wants a drink or to tell him he must drink up. Right now we are practising the sign at the time of drinking—when baby's hand is able to hold the position without the cup actually in it (or you can help him do this) then you make the movement a couple of times each time he has a drink.

(b) Toiletting

Begin now to get baby used to sitting on the floor on the pottie instead of on your lap. He may still like the feel of your arms round him, but this can gradually be dropped although it is still important to stay close to him. Do this before and after feeding times and at bath-time now —these are natural changing times—you need not do this at the odd times when you may find it necessary to change him. Begin now to keep the pottie in the bathroom or toilet and *take baby there to use it.* The fact that baby can begin to relate certain routines with certain places is an important next step, both for his general understanding and for the specific learning we want him to build up about toilet training and his home. It may be cosier to sit him on the pottie in front of the sitting room fire, but he will miss all the wealth of clues taking him to the bathroom to use the pottie will give him. It is where he will ultimately have to go for toiletting, why confuse him by giving him a variety of places now which later are not permitted to be used for this purpose?

You may find he will occasionally, or even regularly for a time, perform when on the pottie, but this is not likely to be maintained as increasing muscle control, change in diet and times of meals, will change performing habits. Don't think of getting baby toilet trained yet—this is still pre-toilet training.

Now we can also begin to set the pattern for our communication sign for going to the toilet. This is a downward movement of your hands on the child's hips—i.e., like pushing down his pants. As soon as the child is familiar with this movement which you do whenever you are about to put him on the pottie, you then take his hands under your own so that he is making the movement with your guidance. Later on we shall expect him to indicate his toiletting needs by making this movement. This is the kind of sign that almost anyone would recognise and this is indeed the intention with all the early communication signs.

(c) Dressing and undressing

To be able to do this for himself requires a child to have quite advanced motor skills, but we can help him on the way here too. He should sit up to be dressed and by now recognise some of the substitute clues we have been giving him—i.e., put his foot out to have his socks and shoes put on when he feels you tap his foot, etc. The awareness of the various parts of his body is a very important part of a baby's early learning. "Body" image, as the experts term this recognition of the form of one's own body, its limits and its abilities which develops as the child becomes aware of his own movements, is too complicated for us to be concerned with here. Perhaps the example of the boy who couldn't follow the command "lie on your back" because he did not know which was his back, will give you some idea of what effect having *no* body image means to a baby. Gently massaging, tickling, slapping, pinching, stroking, blowing on any part of your baby's body when he is undressed all help in teaching this awareness.

Clues for dressing also now become clues for undressing. For example when you want to take off shoes and socks, tap the bottom of baby's shoe. Shoes and hat are usually the first things baby learns to take off for himself and as soon as you feel he is ready begin guiding his hands with your own to do these things (with you behind him, of course). On the whole children learn to take things off for themselves before they learn to put them on for themselves, and we should expect this bias with the deaf/blind.

(d) Sleeping

If your baby is one with a sleeping problem this is likely to show now. By "problem" is generally meant sleeplessness at night when it is disturbing to the rest of the family. The pattern is for the baby to go to sleep very late in the evening and sleep only a couple or so hours after which he wakes and plays, happily but noisily, until he gets bored, hungry or tired when he may become miserable and need some help in getting back to sleep again for the hour or so which remains before it is

22

time to get up. Some drugs are prescribed and help, but this doesn't seem to be the real answer. If this behaviour is due to some effect on the baby of the rubella virus (and it might be) we can only be patient and work out a routine which enables us to cope with this problem until it sorts itself out naturally as it inevitably does. If it is possible baby could be slept in a room where he is unlikely to be heard and an electric baby-listener connected to your bedroom. He is likely to kick off his bedclothes, so dress him warmly, use little cover and keep the room at a reasonable temperature. When he sounds miserable you can pop in, change him and give him a drink, but other than this he should be treated as a normal child should and be left to fall asleep by himself even if this involves a bit of crying. Taking him into your own bed for a bit of peace, or rocking his cot or rubbing his back to get him to sleep may work, but more often than not baby likes it so much he will refuse to go to sleep at any time without it.

The fact that most of these children sleep better once they start school, suggests that the lack of sleep may in some measure be due to lack of stimulation and occupation. If you can give some time to stimulating and occupying your baby whilst he is very young in the ways I am suggesting, I would like to hope that sleeping problems will not be so serious.

Emotional—Becoming one of the family

If your baby is responding to your efforts to help him you have made a good relationship with him—now it is important that he should learn to know and respond to a wider circle of people—daddy, grannie, other children in the family. It is good for other children in the family to help with the handicapped baby's routines where they can. Bringing up this baby should be a family affair and making it such helps to lessen any feelings of jealousy in other children in the family which might arise—it must, however, be an "active" participation, i.e., not just "minding" baby whilst mummy gets on with something else. If possible it should be directly concerned with the baby, but if not then it needs to be something which carries with it some kind of responsibility and for which the child concerned is rewarded.

Baby will benefit from contact with others so long as it comes to him in the way he needs it and you must always explain to others how you do this. He is bound to get cross and frustrated sometimes (all babies do) and you must think of this as a good sign—far better than being passive and apathetic. Do all you can to find out what is causing the frustration and try to put this right first. Sometimes it is just boredom, so distract him by having a romp, or giving him a new toy, a different place to sit in. Frustration is a form of energy which, if you can "channel" it into an activity which provides a learning situation for baby, he will have made good use of instead of wasting. Temper tantrums are

23

not usual at this stage and they will be dealt with in the next booklet.

The need for approval and praise from others is inherent in most of us —we meet this need in the child in the way we show our pleasure at each small new stage he achieves, every time he behaves well or does something properly, in the way we express our affection whether he is good or bad. Few of us realise how vital this is to a child's wanting to achieve more or how much a child comes to behave like others (conform) because he wants to please us. It is very hard to find a reward system (this is what we term it) which is as effective with the deaf /blind baby, but it is just as important for his emotional development as any other baby—maybe more so because he is that much more dependent upon us. If you are aware of this need you will look for ways of making him feel your pleasure in him and what he does—saying "good boy" and patting him on the head is a necessary part of the system, but add to this if you can.

Sensory
(a) Sight
Sometimes needling of the cataracts (if this is the cause of the sight problems) has to be done several times. Although the increase in the light getting to the retina each time may immediately improve the sight, it is usually several weeks before baby learns to use the better sight effectively, i.e., he may have come to recognise a piece of furniture by its shadowy outline, it will take him a little while to recognise that the object he now sees more clearly is the same as that he saw in outline previously. You will get some idea of sight improvement if you watch baby take hold or pick up something he sees—does he judge the size and distance so that he picks it up directly or does he fumble and have to adjust the direction of his hand and grope at the object?

Glasses are often prescribed when the cataracts have been needled in order to perform the function of the pupil which has had to be destroyed because of its opacity. To begin with even just keeping them on the child may be a problem. Sidepieces with holes so that tapes can be used to tie them on at the back are useful. If despite all he keeps taking them off, it's a case of just putting them back each time! The glasses (and hearing aid, of course) must be regarded as part of the daily clothing—to be put on when baby is got up in the morning and taken off when he goes to bed. In these early years glasses are frequently broken and it is advisable, if you can afford it, to have two pairs. These children quickly get used to being without glasses again whilst they are being repaired and once they are back, may object to wearing them all over again.

Often our children are given to the habit of eye-poking—usually at the outer edge. If you see this developing it is advisable to distract him by firmly taking his hand away from the eye and putting something in his hand that he can play with or having a game with him which involves a change of activity. It is possible that this eye-poking gives a pleasurable sensation to the child, but it can harm the eye and quite often bruises the surrounding parts. If it does become a habit, it can take presidence over a more useful occupation. Waving the hand or hands in front of the eyes, necessary in itself as part of the development sequence in connection with focussing also often outlives its usefulness and needs to be turned into a valuable action by putting something "wave-able" into the hand.

(b) Hearing

Up to now the most important thing has been to talk to baby the same as we would talk to any baby but keeping our lips close to his ear or close to the mike of the hearing aid.Remember this is in order that he can use any residual hearing he has and can learn that what he hears comes from you. The words themselves are not as important as the tone in which they are said and the tone is important to emotional development. Now we must deliberately bring other sounds within baby's reach—sounds which, because they come to him in association with something that happens to him frequently and regularly, gradually come to be picked out (like the voice) from other sounds and therefore have meaning for him. An example is banging on the dish with the spoon at meal times. Where there is severe deafness baby must be allowed to feel the vibration of these sounds through his fingers (i.e., fingers on the dish you are banging). If the way he listens suggests he has a reasonable amount of hearing, then say the words "dinner-time" when you are banging the dish—you will see the importance of this as we examine the way a baby learns to talk.

Of course our deaf/blind baby has not been silent all this time—he has been making sounds himself. He cries when he is hungry or has a pain, he coos when he is happy and, as the appropriate muscles develop he will begin to make the usual babbling sounds. Now with the hearing child two things happen to make him keep on babbling—he hears his *own* sounds and he hears mummy imitate them back to him. This stimulates him to go on making more and more complex sounds which eventually become words—but this does not become speech (communication) until what is said has meaning for the child—i.e., he might be able to say the word "milk" but unless he understands that it means the liquid he drinks, it is not speech. A child who hears will hear the word milk many times each day, he is able to ask "what's that" when he sees it in the bottle, in the jug, in a cup or in his own mug —eventually he will say milk when he sees it—but real understanding and communication is only properly achieved when, without the milk actually being in the room, he can say "milk mummy" and know that you can go and get him exactly what he has asked for—this is an example relating to one word—just think how many words there are for a child to know!

This is a very difficult sequence to explain and it will become clearer as we work through, but it is necessary to be aware of it if you want to help a child who neither sees nor hears properly to communicate. It is possible that some will never go beyond signing, but we still must see that they have an opportunity in these early years to experience spoken language and are encouraged to express themselves as far as they are able—however little this is it will take a long long time.

It is likely that our deaf/blind baby does not hear his own babble and therefore does not associate it with the sounds/vibrations mother makes when she babbles back at him as of course, she must. He has to be made aware of his own sounds through ours and we have to give him more clues now than just breath puffs. Speaking is so natural to us that we never think of the complex muscular and breath control that is necessary for the enunciation of a series of rapidly varying sounds which to us are sentences with meaning. Teaching a child to recognise and reproduce speech sounds by means of muscular and breath control (kinesthetic) is a highly skilled job, all we are concerned with now are the babbling sounds and the sort of early speech sounds that babbling develops into in time. An example will show best what I mean —your baby babbles "b b b b b b"—you in turn "b b b b" back to him close to this ear, but in addition you now also put his hand on your lips which make a distinctive movement . . . this tells him *you* are making the sound—how do we tell him he also is making a sound . . . why next time he goes "b b b" put his hand on his own lips . . . and so on. This is a game most of our children love, it can be played any minute of the day for a few minutes and is jolly good when you want to distract his attention.

The following are some of the positions on the face for clues:

m mmmmmmm	hand on cheek
b bbbbbbb	hand on mouth
d dddddddd	hand on mouth
a aaaaaaa (as in car)	hand on throat
r and br	hand on throat
n nnnnnnn	hand on side of nose
p (as in pig)	hand in front of lips

The child will not be able to make or imitate these sounds unless he has the necessary muscular development, but there is no reason why he should not have the experience of them through you to prepare and familiarise him with them in advance. There is a progression from the simple (mmmmmmm) to the more complex (such as "th") and you will find this in detail in the books for teaching the deaf.

26

Our task then, after all that explanation, is to widen the scope of the sounds we bring to baby and help him practice the early speech sounds himself.

Summary

To summarise what goes on at this stage then, we must:

1. Motor—use activities that will encourage
   (a) balance in sitting
   (b) crawling
   (c) pre-walking movements
   (d) holding things

2. Social
   Increase the variety of taste and texture, but do it gradually.
   Begin to use the high chair.
   Take pre-toiletting a stage on.
   See that baby has some sensory experience of what is involved in the everyday routines. As per the example for meal preparation, so for bathing (water from tap, slippery soap, holding toothbrush, brush and comb and so on) dressing, toiletting, etc.

3. *Emotional*—
   Increase time and variety of special play with mother and widen the circle of people with whom he comes into daily contact.

4. *Sensory*—
   Encourage him to use any sight he possesses by looking for shiny or brightly coloured things.
   Bring to his notice some sounds (other than voice) which he can associate with what is happening to him.
   Let him touch and smell things used in routines.
   Touch him and encourage him to touch himself so that he learns about his own body.

5. *Communication*—begin to use communication signs for
   (a) expressing your pleasure in him (pat his head).
   (b) toiletting (downward movement on hips).
   (c) drinking (hand movement used in raising cup to lips).
   Imitate babbling sounds, giving baby the feel of these through his hands on your face and throat. Let him feel his own sounds by putting his hands on his face and throat.

You will see now that the length of each chapter and the summary of each is increasing. This is what is happening to your baby—one thing is leading to two others and his awareness of the world he lives in, the people who care for him, and what he himself can do is gradually

27

broadening. Some of these things he will have accomplished and some he still has to be encouraged and helped with for some considerable time yet. You can be certain that everything he has learned has been a lot harder for him than for the normal child and therefore whatever the stage he has reached overall, you can be jolly proud of him.

All the movement practice which we have encouraged has to be worked through before our child can learn to walk by himself—all the listening and recognising sounds, using sight touch smell and the feel of things to him are necessary preliminaries to the greater knowledge of the world that is open to our child once he can walk about by himself. One could well say that it is of little use being able to walk around unless you are able to use your sensory abilities to learn about all the new things there are to explore once you can get about on your own.

We shall play an increasing part in helping our child from now on. You must accept and prepare for this because you know that if you help now intensively for perhaps a period of a year or so, your child is more likely to respond to the educational help that will then be available to him—once at school you will still need to help him when he is at home, but you will not have so much to teach and initiate new things, rather to provide the opportunities for practice.

CHAPTER 5
NEW PERSPECTIVES

We now enter a new and exciting period of the deaf/blind child's life —one of supreme importance to him and possibly the most exacting for you, his parents. In terms of normal development we can consider this period as starting from standing alone and working towards readiness for education or training. Because of the uneven rate of development likely to occur in any one sequence compared to another, and, consequently, considerable overlapping from previous chapters and within the new ones, it is best to take each area separately and describe the path along which you must encourage your child to travel in that particular area.

This is the period of life when children learn more, and learn more quickly, than at any other time. A deaf/blind child will never learn it all, so we must make sure that what he does learn is useful to him. A deaf /blind child will take things in more slowly and his retardation will become more and more obvious, so we must be careful not to pressure him. Some of the sequences set out in the following Chapters will extend for most deaf/blind children up to 8 or 9 years of age, or may never be achieved entirely on their own, but they provide the guidelines for continued progress.

The areas we must have in mind now are:
Communication
Social Training
Motor Skills
Mobility
Emotional Development
Play and Learning

These headings differ from those previously used, but the following few words of explanation will enable you to see why it is now important to group them this way. Once again I must stress that it is essential you remember that no one area develops in isolation, they are all interrelated and interdependent. Lack of development in one area may delay another, progress in another may hurry one that is slow.

Communication
We must work through from the primitive kind of communication we

have so far used to meaningful natural gestures and we must decide which alternative method of communication will best utilise our child's abilities so that we can use this to build on towards a higher level of communication. Our aim must be to get from the stage of giving information to the child to that where he can begin to give us (or ask for from us) very simple information. We now have to give him better tools and then provide him with the opportunity to use them —so that he finds communicating a necessity initially and a habit eventually.

Social Training

Learning *How* to behave is just as important a part of social training as is learning self-care. Sometimes we as parents get so involved with the latter that we forget the former. It is easier to pick up our child's clothes from the floor for him than to stop and teach him to put them in a pile on a chair; easier to let him get down from the table when he is finished than teach him to wait until the others are also finished. There are, nevertheless, things that he will have to learn to do sometimes, so why allow him to develop a pattern of behaviour which he is later going to have to unlearn—why not learn the more acceptable behaviour right from the first? So in this Chapter we will look at social behaviour as well as the skills of self-care for which, in this period, feeding, washing, toiletting, dressing and undressing sequences will be completed to the point of independence.

Motor Skills and Mobility

Although mobility is dependent upon motor skills, it now needs to be seen as a separate skill. Mobility means getting about for a purpose rather than just moving about or just movement for the joy of it, important as these are for all children. It is the foundation of independence for all severely handicapped children, but particularly for the deaf/blind who lack the incentives provided by sight and hearing which motivate children to move purposefully. Now is the time to take the first steps to mobility and few will do this without deliberate training and encouragement from us. We must establish mobility within the home environment by methods which will be useful to him when he moves on to new and more demanding environments i.e. school, visiting etc.

Emotional Development

Even given continuing love, security, acceptance, encouragement and firm handling, some emotional problems are inevitable in a child for whom eye-contact, facial expression, voice tones and language for reasoning are missing. These problems cannot be anticipated because they arise from what is going on at the time and their solution depends on the particular circumstances at that time. But we can look at the sequence in which the emotions generally develop and at some of the emotional problems that can arise, the causes and suggest some ways in which we can try to lessen the effect on both the child and the family.

Play and Learning

Up to now we have mainly been concerned with encouraging our child through play to learn to use his sensory channels so far as he is able —now we want to show him how to use these sensory channels to gather the kind of information that will provide him with knowledge about his world, the people in it and the events that occur in it. Providing the kind of material and experience that will be both meaningful and useful to him is going to stretch our ingenuity to the extreme. It is more than just the right choice, it is also provision in the right order so that what he learns grows in complexity and variety.

Although reciprocal play begins between child and parents, family and friends must also be shown how to play with the deaf/blind child. At some time your child may have a home teacher who will become a regular visitor or, if nursery school provision has increased as we hope it is going to do, he may be able to attend a preschool class. In the event of the latter, specific learning routines will be provided at the school and at home you will need to play a complementary role and play the same way, but with different sets of materials. Hence the Chapter on Play and Learning is divided into two parts, the first concerned with early play routines and the second will set out alongside each other play schemes for use in preschool groups and at home. If your child is not in a preschool class, you can work through the preschool or home schemes, if he is then you will use only the home schemes under the guidance of the teacher.

Priorities

It is not possible to give priority order to the areas with which we are concerned, they are all equally important. Communication, of course, pervades all activities as indeed does emotional development. Of the areas that require deliberate training the amount of time you can devote to giving individual attention to your child may determine the proportion given to any one area. Social training is vital to personal independence—being able to dress and undress himself, manage toileting and washing on his own and being able to feed himself not only lessens work and time for you, but makes your child socially acceptable, prepares him for school, but above all, are the achievements on which his own self-confidence depends. So I would suggest that the greater amount of time should be spent on social training and every

31

advantage taken of the opportunities it offers to teach and practice communication.

Try in addition to have as long a period each day as you can spare (5 minutes is better than not at all) for some deliberate mobility training. Several brief play periods during which you can share a planned learning experience and some fun-and-games in the form of a romp or shared physical activity are essential every day, the former increasing in length of time as the child's interest in play for learning grows and he is able to sit and attend for longer periods.

It may be better for you—it is certainly better for your child, if these periods can be at the same time each day. Events happening regularly, as I have explained, provide the deaf/blind child with his only means of monitoring time. When his anticipation is fulfilled he derives a sense of security that at this stage is very important to him. This may sound as if it will tie you and the family to one place, but whilst the activity and time need to be the same, what is done need not necessarily be in the same place. If you are skilful in choosing your tactile clues, these will provide the stability rather than this coming from the place where events occur. For example, if a brief touch of the table, plate and cutlery provide the clues for mealtimes, these are just the same whether you are at home, at school, or taking a meal with a friend or in a restaurant. If a touch of the pottie means toiletting, take his pottie with you when you go out (it can be used in the car, in a public toilet, a friend's toilet etc)—he will recognise it for its use. If he uses a proper toilet, as long as the clue is touching a part that is common to all toilets, he will recognise it. The things you can use for motor training period can be found in a friend's house just as easily as your own and provide a good opportunity for that friend to see how well your child does or how hard he tries, or even how hard it is for him to do it at all.

Mobility training in its early stages must be done at home because home is where mobility begins and from whence it must grow outwardly—rather like the ripple from the pebble thrown into the pond. However if this has to be left out on high days and holidays and it is the only thing that does get left out, you will have done jolly well.

As I have said, this period of your deaf/blind child's life is going to make heavy demands on you. I hope you will have good relatives and friends who will see to it that you have some free time—without any shadow of doubt for every hour you spend working with your child NOW you will be likely to have two hours of extra freedom later on.

CHAPTER 6
COMMUNICATION

The ability to communicate by speech develops in children so naturally that we hardly ever give a thought to how it comes about. The average child who is of normal intelligence, lives in a happy talking family environment, who hears and sees the people he is communicating with, their facial expressions and can also see the things that are being talked about understanding by $2\frac{1}{2}$ years most of the simple language spoken to him, can say 3 word sentences and can give us simple information.
To do this he has:

(i)   to be able to hear and want to listen to what he hears (if he is not interested in what he hears, he will not necessarily hear);

(ii) to be able to understand the meaning of what he hears which means he must have the ability to distinguish between different speech sounds, combinations of speech sounds and sequences of speech sounds and be able to associate them with the person, object or event to which they refer (if what he hears has no meaning for him, a child will eventually stop paying attention to what he hears);
and
to be able to relate what he has understood from the speech he has heard to his own knowledge in order to determine if and how he should respond, and this depends upon how intelligent he is and how much he has learned;

(iii) once a response has been thought out, he has to put this into the right kind of language sequence and organise the nerves, muscles rhythm, intonation etc, that allow him to give expression to speech sounds that are meaningful to others.

All other means of communication must contain the above three elements (i) receiving, (ii) comprehending (inner language) and (iii) expressing. If (i) does not occur neither (ii) nor (iii) can possibly occur, i.e. to communicate you must have something to communicate about.
It has to be accepted that learning to communicate by speech in the normal manner is out of the question for a child whose two main channels for receiving information are inefficient. He will need teaching in a

special way, but which one of the several ways depends on the degree of the dual handicap. We all have to progress through certain levels in order to develop communication by words, whether these words are spoken or signed. Should a deaf/blind child be unable to reach this highest level, he must be encouraged to reach the highest he can.

Levels of Communication

1. Signalling—The child can lead you to a place where something he needs is kept (fridge for milk), will put your hand on something he wants manipulated for him (a button done up, a toy car wound up) will anticipate events from clues in the environment (sits to table when is aware of table being set). At this level communication is related to something actually present at the time, the child is not holding pictures, words, signs or any other kind of representative inner thought in his mind. Some deaf /blind children remain at this stage and whilst it is useful and better than no communication at all, it is obvious that it severely limits social, emotional and intellectual development. In the earlier chapters we have been at pains to provide our child with the kind of clues that will help him to anticipate things happening to him—this level of communication demonstrates an awareness of these clues and leads on to:

2. *Gross Signs and Gesturing*—Several simple gross signs were introduced earlier for drinking, toiletting etc, but what is important now is that we teach the child to do these so that he is being introduced to communication as a two-way process. Natural gestures are the movements a child makes to express something in his mind for which he yet has no word (he spreads his arms wide to tell us how big something is). It shows that thoughts are forming in his mind and that he wants to communicate these to you. He may or may not have to see others make these movements, but they are used by him spontaneously. The appearance of natural gestures is an indication of potential for language and a readiness for us to begin to teach this by signing or speech as follows:

3. *Sign Systems*   A. Systematic Sign Language plus manual alphabet. Need partial sight—may be able to read large print and to write.

                               B. Manual alphabet. Blind or only light /darkness Braille reading and writing.

      Speech   C. Tadoma Vibration Method. Blind or partially sighted.

A. The *Systematic Sign Language* (SSL) used in this country is the Paget and it consists of signs made by the hands and fingers, movements of the hands and arms and by the position these are held in relation to the body. It has the advantage over the sign system used by the deaf in that it teaches the natural flow and rhythm of speech and the construction, grammar and tenses match with reading and writing. It is a little difficult to learn at first and you need to be properly instructed—you do not need to learn it all at once, you have to know the basic factors and learn a new sign so that you can perform it fluently before introducing it to the child. There are no signs for proper names, so these are finger spelt. The Paget system is being used increasingly in deaf/blind units now and the children taught by this method seem to communicate more freely and earlier than when taught by finger spelling only—but such children do have a reasonable degree of sight.

B. The Manual Alphabet (MA) used for finger spelling in this country is the two handed one. The speaker spells the letter shapes or positions on to the hand of the child who in turn spells back on the speaker's hand. It is very easy to learn and in time can be used at speed. A one-hand alphabet is used in the US in which the position of the fingers of the hand indicate the letter and it is "read" by the listener cupping his hand over that of the speaker. Finger spelling has the disadvantage that you cannot converse at a distance, across a room or on the telephone (although for this a morse code key might have application) but it is useful in a cinema or a church.

C. The *Tadoma (Vibration) Method* is used in the US. The child places his hand on the speaker's face with the thumb lightly on the lips and the fingers spread on the cheek and upper neck. He learns to "speech read" the vibrations and in turn, by placing his hand on his own face, to reproduce the vibrations and speech. If your child enjoys feeling the vibrations as you speak it is an excellent thing to encourage for it is a source of valuable clues. As a method by itself it is most successful with the more intelligent children.

These levels of communication provide us with a guide to the sequence through which we should now work. Our long term aim must be to reach some degree of competency in one of the two sign systems. We must continue to talk to our children alongside whatever other method we use, because even if they cannot use speech to reply, they may get valuable tone and vibration clues. Also it is often possible to learn some speech after a sign language has been learned and we should be on the look out for signs of increased understanding of speech due to growing awareness of the existence of communication. Obviously we must encourage any attempt at sounds that the child himself may make.

Gross Signs and Natural Gestures

To teach your child to do the gross signs, you must first make the sign to him, then guide his hands (with yours over his) through the movement of the sign. As he gets to recognise it you will begin to feel the beginnings of reciprocal movements of his hands under yours and this is when you stop guiding him and let him make the sign but with your hands over his. When his movements are correct and sure, then you can take your hands away and let him copy it of his own accord once you have given him the pattern. Natural gestures are useful to us all, pointing, waving bye-bye, patting the tummy when hungry etc, movements mostly with hands and arms, but also with faces. Pointing in particular is important. It gives him a means of explaining something at a distance from it, without having to lead you to it. It can be taught through many games, throwing a ball, pointing to where it landed, going after it, throwing and pointing again. After doing it together, take it in turns to throw so that he has to tell you by pointing where to go and pick up the ball, the car he has pushed, the brick he has hidden, his brother hiding, and so on.

Sign System

Now let us see what the sign methods must contain to match up with the normal language. In all that follows in the rest of this Chapter the word "sign" will mean whichever of the alternative methods you have chosen.

Normal Child	Deaf/Blind Child
1. Hearing and listening to speech.	Receiving a sign.
2. Understanding and relating to own experience.	Recognising the sign because he has received it before and has associated it with a similar object or event.
3. Imitating sound sequences heard before in a similar context.	Imitating the sign received before in a similar context.
4. As a result of retaining 1, 2 and 3 above, expressing himself in 3	Also as a result of 1, 2 and 3 being retained, he can imitate the sign in order to get some-

36

without 1 and 2 hap-
pening, i.e. he can ask
for or give information of
his own accord.

thing or identify something.

We shall introduce the sign system we decide to use in the following
sequence: (i)   Sign imitation games.
             (ii)   Transfer of gross signs to sign system.
             (iii) Introduction of new items in sign system.

Sign Imitation Games

Both the MA and the SSL demand a considerable degree of dexterity
and imitation skill which it would take a small child some time to develop. A child would not be able to imitate a fine finger movement with
any degree of accuracy until well after the age when he could speak.
Try to think at what age a child will point to "the little finger on the
right" at the end of the song "One two three four five" and know that it
is the right one or be able to lift one finger at a time when the others
are kept down. Therefore we begin the imitation games with copying
gross movements and gradually refine the movements down from
body, legs and arms to both hands together, then one hand at a time,
then fingers all together and thumb separate and finally individual
fingers. These overlap of course and the degree of skill and speed of
development will depend on the chronological age of your child. He
may already have reached an age when he can make the finer movements and so will go through the gross imitation stage more quickly.
There are plenty of children's games which do exactly what you want
your child to learn so other children can be brought in to make the
learning more fun. "Here we go round the mulberry bush" has infinite
variations for the movements we can do, many of which should be becoming meaningful to the child as signs he has learned, brushing his
hair, eating, etc and can be interspersed with new movements which
you will help him copy, stamping his feet, waving bye-bye, pointing a
finger, clapping his hands etc. etc. The Hoky Coky song is another
good imitation game using different parts of the body.
Your child will need to learn not only to copy in this general game situation but also in a one to one relationship. The "One two three four
five" song about the fish and "Round and round the garden" and "This
little pig" are bringing the child and you into direct contact with hands
and fingers and they draw attention to the different fingers as you
count each one in turn. Encourage him gradually to do this more and
more on his own.
The next stage is to copy just one movement, not as a familiar sequence in a game but specifically as copying. This is best done standing in front of a full length mirror (if your child has enough sight to

37

benefit from this at close range) with you standing immediately behind your child with your arms on each side of him at first and then alongside him. He can then both see your movements on the side of his body and with the hand that you want him to use. If you stand opposite he will use the wrong hand. Begin with big movement stamping your feet, waving one arm then the other, shaking your head, nodding your head (more useful natural gestures). Gradually refine movements down to making shapes, first a big hole with your arms meeting above your head to look through, gradually getting smaller and smaller till you can put finger and thumb together to look through, put your whole arms straight up, then your hands, then two fingers, then two different fingers then two on the same hand. Point to your eyes, your nose, your knees, your hands then different parts of your hands and fingers.

When your child can do this he is ready for Paget or finger spelling, but please realise that this will take a very long time, maybe years. This is not to say that you cannot introduce the MA or SSM before he can copy with such accuracy. He may be able to begin to understand just as a child hears and understands long before he develops the muscular skills required of him to speak himself. He is babbling while you are talking. The deaf/blind child is learning movement, and we hope sometimes playing with the movements himself, while you are giving him the language for which he will require these skills when he is ready to use them. (That's a nice confusing sentence to finish with)!

Transfer of Gross Signs and Gestures to Signs

To do this we give the gross sign and follow this immediately with the sign. The child gives the gesture you match it with the sign. When the sign is accepted and returned, we can drop out the gross sign and use the sign only. You might perhaps compare this process to the hearing child's use of "choochoo" before "train".

Use of Signs Only

Once all the gross signs have been transferred to signs, new "words" can be given directly in signs.

Language Scheme

There are no hard and fast rules about which words you should teach first. The examples I am about to give are mainly for guidance and if you wish to make a plan relative to your own particular circumstances, this is fine. But do make a plan and go through it systematically for this is vital to success. Also it must be done regularly within the daily routine or it will not be remembered.

To get through this scheme could take 2 years or 10. It might well represent the total of what a deaf/blind child could ever learn, but with

38

SUGGESTED LANGUAGE SCHEME

Within Routine	Word	Gross Sign to ⟶	Paget or MA	New Sign Sequence
Meals	eat	Touch bunched fingertips to lips	eat	more ⟶ spoon / fork / plate / cup ⟶ biscuits / cake / bread / etc
	drink	Hand cupped to shape of cup and lifted towards mouth	drink	gone
Dressing and Undressing		Tapping on limb required to move for putting on or taking off	body parts	Names of garments ⟶ fastenings
Toilet		Rubbing hips as if taking down pants	loo or lav	
Washing		Rub hands together	wash	soap, towel, water, tap plug, etc
Bath		Hands rubbed down body from shoulders	bath	
Brush		Feel position and size of bristles	teeth hair	
Motor Activities	up	Tap under elbow	up	
	down	Tap on shoulder with downward push	down	car (for ride in one)
	walk	Run your finger and thumb in walking movement down child's palm	walk	swim swing
	jump	Take both hands and move up and down	jump	
Occupation	play	Put child's hands round plaything and give them a little pat	play	Name of object of occupation

General	Gross Sign — to	Paget or MA	New Sign Sequence
Mummy	Whatever signs you have chosen to alert the child it is you	mum	names of members of family and then of friends etc with whom child is likely to come into contact frequently
Daddy		dad	
Yes	Child feels your head nodding approval	yes	—
No	Double pat on back of hand	no	—
Please	Hands clasped over each other fingers together	please	thanks
Hallo	Your own choice of sign could be handshake	hallo	goodbye, goodnight
Hot	Take child's hand and make a quick movement away from hot object + 'no' sign	hot	cold
Wait	Hands clasped together with fingers interlocked	wait	come
Fun and Games Signs for play activities	Patting thighs = adult swings round with child in arms; Hands over hands = roll over on floor	swing	jump, run, skip, dance etc.

only this much at his "fingertips" he would be able to ask for a familiar person, for food, drink, warmth, clothes, bath, toilet, a walk or ride and for the things he liked doing. If this scheme has been completed by the time a child joins preschool training, he has a good chance of continued growth of language in its more complex form.

How to use the signs

A. Give the child the sign at the same time as he is in contact with relevant object.
B. Give the sign.
   Let child feel the object or something connected with what he is to do (e.g. touch plate or food when you have signed "eat").
   Help him imitate the sign then let him have the object or get on with doing what is involved.
C. Give the sign.
   Let the child feel the object or something connected with what he is to do.
   Give him the initial movement towards imitating the sign and let him finish it himself. Do this several times before you offer help and when he does do it alone, give him plenty of praise.
   Let him have object etc.
D. This is where you are watchful for even the tiniest sign made by the child of his own accord and when you see it, reward him with the object or event. Even if this means giving him a bath at the wrong time of the day, you say? To begin with, yes, for it is of supreme importance that he comes to realise that signing is just not a game only, but is a tool he can use to make the things he wants happen, to have his needs satisfied. In the first place his needs are basic, like needing a drink because you are thirsty—later these are much more complex like needing to know something, to share information, to receive sympathy, to chat to someone or join in a group. You need a lot of language to fulfil such needs all of which a deaf/blind child will have at some time despite his handicaps and over which he will become frustrated when he cannot find a way to communicate them to others. Providing you do it carefully and you do know that your child can imitate the appropriate sign, you can withhold an object or event until the sign has been made. If you decide to use this with a child who is reluctant to give signs, you must stick to your guns and not relent and give in, otherwise he will not benefit from the experience.

Points to keep in mind in using sign language

(a) A child who sees and hears you has you in close contact—you must also have this close contact with the deaf/blind child and of necessity it has to be physical, i.e. bodily contact. For the very

41

young child this means having him on your lap with your face near his whenever possible. When communication is established this contact is maintained with the vibration method by his hand on your face and with finger-spelling by the touch of your hand spelling on to his.

(b) Language development and intellectual development go hand in hand. It is thought that there is a definite stage in a child's development when things acquire permanence—before this if you let him see you hide a toy under a cushion he makes no effort to find it because so far as he is concerned it no longer exists. This suggests that at that stage he can only hold things in his mind when they are actually there and it is obvious that this will apply to a deaf /blind child for a longer time than the normal child and stresses the need, when you begin signing, for him to feel the object *Whilst You* are signing. Only later on when you think he associates the sign and object can you sign and then give him the object to feel. Once the child can do it for himself in the right context you can use signs as a warning that an event is going to happen, i.e. when he must leave his toys to have his dinner you will sign "eat" and you will sign it again when his meal is put in front of him.

(c) Remember communication has to be a pleasurable experience and for this reason the choice of initial signs we teach must be related to something the child likes or enjoys—if he is a poor feeder "eat" is definitely not the first word to be introduced.

(d) Remember how many times a non-handicapped child must hear words before he can use them, remember he has heard and seen others communicating for at least 18 months, before he begins to hold a conversation. Remember also that he practices it on himself (some believe this is the basis for inner language). Because of these things and because a sign language is not so efficient for thinking as speech, be patient with the deaf/blind child and expect the start to be a very slow one.

(e) Some tips for making signing more comfortable:
Warm hands and short fingernails for MA.
Once the child knows your name, sign your name when you go to him after an absence.
Know your signs accurately, if you falter it will confuse the child.
If he is tired or not fit, don't expect too much of him.
If you are using Paget make sure you are in front of the child and at his level.

(f) Remember always to speak while you are signing.

Finally—now that we have examined communication and language as a separate entity use the findings only for reference. Language is not and cannot be separate, it permeates every aspect of a child's life as indeed does the need to communicate. This chapter has been intended to stress the importance of communication and to show you how to substitute a sign language for speech, but it must not be taught in isolation. It is the core of all the rest of work with your child and it is vital to him throughout all his life. Maintaining and increasing auditory awareness remains a very important part of our total approach to the deaf/blind child. Auditory training programmes are provided in the Chapter 11 Play and Learning Part 2.

CHAPTER 7

SOCIAL TRAINING

1. Dressing and Undressing

So far it is we who have taken off and put on our child's clothing, watching for him to show some recognition of the sequence by making anticipatory moves—i.e. holding out his foot for his socks and shoes when we have tapped his feet. He may well have discovered for himself how to get shoes and socks off, this is fine but what we now want to do is teach these skills systematically by taking advantage of the opportunities offered every day when he gets up in the morning, goes to bed at night and goes outdoors and comes indoors. Before going into detail, it helps if you:

(a)   Dress and undress your child consistently—i.e. put things on and take them off always in the same order.

(b)   Always use the same sequence of movements appropriate to each garment.

(c)   Break down the movements the child requires to make to put on or take off a garment into a sequence of small steps which the child can learn to do himself one at a time, i.e. taking off a bonnet involves:
  (i)   moving hand up to head
  (ii)   grasping the bonnet with one hand
  (iii) pulling bonnet off head
  Teach (iii) first, then (ii) and (iii) and finally (i) plus (ii) and (iii). This pattern has to become established in the child's brain by repetition every time he wears a bonnet before he will be able to perform it automatically by himself.

(d)   Teach one garment at a time.

(e)   Use clothing which can be put on and taken off easily. When possible use zips or velcro instead of buttons, as it is easier to teach pulling these up and down than buttoning and unbuttoning which require very fine finger control. Tight clothing is difficult to get on and off—have clothing too big rather than too small.

(f)   Dress him from behind and with his hands under yours—on your lap, on the floor or standing.

(g)   Allow plenty of time—guard against helping him simply because you are in a hurry.

(h)   Once he has shown you he can do some part for himself, try not to

44

do it for him again. Obviously when a child is ill or very tired he needs help as would any child, but at all other times let him do it by himself once he knows how.

(i) Talk to him about what you are doing, what he is doing and tell him why and what he must do—use the communication method you have decided upon to convey the names of the garments (coat etc) the limb they go on (arm etc) and the action he must perform (pull, push, up, down, over etc). (Refer Chapter on Communication).

(j) Try out each procedure yourself with your own clothes so that you know exactly what it is you are trying to get over to your child.

(k) Always show your pleasure and approval for a good try as well as for success.

(l) Touching the bath or the bed is the signal for "it is *time* to undress". Touching the pile of clothes to be put on is the signal for "it is *time* to dress".

(m) Let your child feel his clothes being folded and placed in a pile when he takes them off—place the clothes for the next day in a similar pile, but remember the items must be in the correct dressing order.

(n) It will help your child get the idea of right side and wrong side if you help him turn sleeves on whole garments that he reverses while undressing and if you always give him his clothes right side out when dressing.

(o) Sew tabs in the back of all garments, let him feel these to identify the back whilst learning to dress so that these will be known clues when he takes over the task on his own.

(p) Remember the communication aspect is as important as the skills. Once "take off your . . ." is understood, you can teach "put on your . . ." When both actions and signals are learned, if he takes something off at an inappropriate moment (shoes and hats frequently are) you can *tell* him to put it back on. You can welcome such opportunities as time for practice for communication and you can have lots of fun and good rapport at the same time.

Occasionally we encounter special problems in connection with dressing and undressing. A child may be able to take off his clothes well and quickly, but only at the wrong times. It may be a sign of craving for attention because undressing is a time associated with getting attention. Or it may be that he wants to be left alone and he has learned that when he is undressed he is generally not expected to do anything. Or it may be that something is too tight, is uncomfortable, is rubbing, or if it is the shoe that comes off, maybe there is a little stone in it—all these things must be investigated because a child without communication can only tell us of his difficulties in this way. It is rarely naughtiness—understanding his needs and putting things right is the

45

quickest and surest way to achieving normal behaviour.

Undressing

Children learn to take off before they learn to put on—it's easier.

Tackle each and every garment as the example given for the bonnet —that is *you* take off up to the last movement of the sequence (i.e. pants down to the ankles) then taking the child's hands in yours, take him through the movement required to complete the taking off. Watch for him to make some move to do this himself and notice if, under your hands, he is making some of the effort of taking off himself. When you are certain you feel this, this is the moment when you must begin to lessen your help and, still keeping your hands under his, let him begin to take over. When you think he is ready to do more for himself (i.e. pulling pants down from the knees) show him how to manage the new bit and leave him to finish the previously learned bit by himself.

Some tips for making undressing easier:

1. Trousers, pants, pyjama pants

    Hook child's thumbs over elastic or band, squeezing his hands over this and pushing them down.

2. Vest, jumper

    Taking these items up just far enough for them to be covering the face is usually encouragement enough for the child to pull it right off to free his face. Making the first step can be helped by crumpling the bottom of the vest or jumper a little so that the child's hands have something firm to hold and pull over the shoulders. His hands then grasp opposite sides, and his arms come up as vest is brought over head and finally pulled off over bent elbows.

3. Dresses and nightdresses

    Take off downwards.

4. Cardigans, shirts, pyjama-tops

    You must undo the buttons for some time—he is unlikely to learn to do this before the next stage, the preschool period. Take off one sleeve and teach him the second one first because it is easier when the rest of the garment is free. Hold the bottom of the sleeve and ease off, encouraging the child to pull away from you and draw his arm free. Treat both sleeves this way and finally teach him to hold the bottom of the sleeve with the opposite hand and pull free for himself.

5. Coat, dressing gown

    This can be done as for the shirt, but when child is physically able, it is better to teach him to grasp the lapels and ease the coat off the shoulders.

6. Boots

    Pull off heel for him, let him finish.

46

Dressing

This is not easy, so take it slowly. Go step by step, last step first.

1. Socks

    Fold toe of sock into itself, put over child's foot, roll sock on and pull up. The child first pulls up sock from ankle, next he pulls it from below the ankle and up, taking hold of the sock by putting thumbs between sock and leg/foot and grasping it. Next teach child to look/feel for the hole at the end of the sock so that he can roll it up over his foot and complete the whole task of pulling on. Finally teach him to take hold of the sock between thumb and fingers and guide his toes into the turned in toe-piece.

2. Shoes

    Left shoe:
    1. Grasp shoe with left thumb under the shoe tongue. Grasp inside back of shoe with right thumb inside and fingers outside.
    2. Leg is crossed in front of child with sole facing the right.
    3. Foot is placed between child's hands directly in front of shoe opening.
    4. Slip toes in and then heel.

    Reverse procedure for right shoe.

3. Pants, trousers, pyjama legs

    Some of this training needs to be done with him on your knee or with him sitting on the floor, but as soon as possible stand child in front of you, facing away from you, his back supported by leaning against you. With your arms in front of him giving him support against you, bend over making him bend forward also (making sure his knees bend). Holding his pants in your left hand tap his left leg with your right hand then lift it from the floor and guide through the leg hole. Similarly with the right side. If the child's balance is poor, he may not like this, so give him time to get used to bending before you start on the training. To train him he must grasp the elastic or band as for pulling off and he must be shown how to pull them on over his hips, then up over knees, and hips, then from ankles all the way up and finally he must learn to find the leg holes and pull them up all by himself. Remember this part of dressing is tied up with motor training—one helps the other.

4. Vest, jumper, slipover dress

    Put the neck of the garment over the child's head, help him find the armholes (both at once is easier than two movements) then pull it down and on. His first task is to pull it down once the arms are through—if you just leave it across the chest, the child generally may find out how to pull it for sheer comfort. The next step

47

of pulling down from over his face he may also do spontaneously. To enable him to put it on by himself finally you will need to give it to him with the bottom open and slightly rolled so he has something to grasp. This little rolled portion does become his clue to what to do with this type of clothing.

5. Shirt, pyjama top, cardigan, coat, dressing gown

Help your child grasp the right shoulder with his left hand or the reverse if he is left handed. Help him push his arm down the sleeve, pull high onto the right shoulder. Help him feel for the left armhole and hold coat while he pushes his arm through. Put his hands on yours whilst you do the buttons so that he learns that something has to happen to fasten the coat. An alternative method is to put the coat, cardigan etc on a table, outside down, collar nearest child. Child puts both arms into sleeves and brings coat over head to put on. This is a hard sequence to learn and I would advise you to do it all for him for quite a time so that he becomes aware of the various directions his body must be turned. Provide him with clues about texture, weight, collar, buttons of the coat so that he comes to recognise it in relation to going out—link it with his hat. Also let him feel your coat after he has his on, let him feel you putting yours on so that he knows you are going with him and also wear a coat.

6. Useful aids

Dressing and undressing a large doll.

Watching and helping other children dressing.

Montessori type frames for learning about buttons, zips, hooks, belt buckles—you can make these for yourself.

2. Toilet Training

By now, and with a bit of luck, our deaf/blind child is prepared at least to sit on his pottie as a matter of habit and without a fuss. To train him to use it we need also to be systematic and above all to have patience and optimism. Step number 1 is to take the child out of nappies—in my experience a child never becomes fully toilet trained until this is done. Putting them into pants may mean a lot of mopping up for a short while but if it means earlier training and not having a child's legs spread out by the bulk of the nappie when he is learning to walk, and above all not having him still wearing nappies long after they should have been discarded, it's well worth it. Pants are more uncomfortable than nappies when wet, he will be made aware of what has happened if his legs and feet are also uncomfortable. Pants are easily changed also more easily washed and dried than nappies. Also so far as self-help is concerned you can begin teaching taking pants on and off —something that cannot be done by the child in a nappie—and a child cannot be independent in his toiletting until he can manage his pants for himself.

So I would hope that once your child can stand alone, no more nappies will be used in the daytime.

Let me say again here that being able to control these bodily functions requires a certain stage of development which these children are often slower to reach than normal children. This means we must be prepared for a longish period of training, but it does not mean that we should delay the training. As with the other training schedules, you plan what you are going to do and stick firmly to that plan—it soon becomes habit and you find yourself doing it without thinking about it. The most successful plan I know is first to write down the times during the day when your child is wet. Do this for at least 10 days and you will find that there are several times a day when your child is regularly wet —from now on pot him every day just *before* these times. This way you can be certain of "catching" him sometimes and this is your chance to show him what he has done and reward him with a sweetie or a special toy which is kept only for this purpose. It is from this kind of beginning that toilet training develops. Do not start the child on the big toilet until he is using the pottie regularly—use a small seat over the big one to begin with and fix a small rail (or toilet roll holder) where the child can hold on to it if he is a little afraid of falling off to begin with. Having a small stool to support his feet if you find this helps, is also a good idea. Being toilet trained is not something which happens naturally, normal children learn to do this as much because it pleases their parents and because it is something everyone else does, as for any reason of cleanliness or comfort. With the deaf/blind child it is the regularity of the pattern of the routine and the rewards connected with it that make it a desirable thing to do—so it is easy to see that getting cross with him in any toiletting situation will be harmful and delay success. An accident is an accident—when it happens do the toilet sign and take him *immediately* to the bathroom to change his pants, don't grumble, but don't praise—accept it calmly and this will reassure him.

It helps if you:
1. Stay with your child if possible whilst he is getting used to a new position.
2. Never keep a child on the pottie more than 10 minutes.
3. Do not give him things to eat or drink while on the pottie.
4. Toilet only in the bathroom or separate toilet, except in the very early stages when it is useful to have a pottie handy to catch him if he's beginning to indicate the need but not quickly enough. Regular potting must be in bathroom or toilet.
5. Use the appropriate signs before going to the bathroom and when the child sits on the toilet (i.e. need two signs).

49

6. Once a little boy stands alone, let him stand to the toilet (on something secure if necessary to bring him high enough).
7. Dabble a little cold water on your child's hand (or put his hands into a little bowl of water) to encourage him to perform, but use this only in the early stages.
8. Be patient. Don't get depressed or anxious if it takes a long time to achieve.
9. Remember that being dry at night is usually the last step to full toilet training—regulating the flow of liquids towards the evening sometimes helps the older child and there are some electric appliances which can assist if bedwetting persists.
10. Remember that regular toilet habits depend on a proper food and drink intake. If there are feeding problems, toilet training is more difficult to achieve.
11. *Problems*
    The child who does not perform in the bathroom but waits until he has left it so late he wets or soils his pants, has in fact, learned to control "not going". He is getting some idea of what is wanted and this is a normal stage through which all children go. Treat this by continuing to take him on schedule and be lavish with the praise when he gets there on time. There are times when this is deliberate naughtiness and if this is so, he must be treated as any other normal child in such circumstances.

3. Washing etc

By now bathing should have become a recognised and enjoyed routine. It should be possible to make the transition to the big bath at this stage and this provides an opportunity to start teaching your child to wash himself. A big bath is less frightening if at first mummy or a big sister/brother gets in with him and sitting behind him guides him through the actions of washing himself. He will enjoy rubbing his tummy first. There is likely to be some resistance, particularly if he wants to play. Gradually increase the amount of washing that is done before play and when you can complete the job without resistance then begin encouraging him to take over a bit at a time as in the previous routines. Decide upon and stick to the same routine, i.e. if you wash his hands first, then face and body parts after, then always do it in this order, and let him learn it in this order. Ultimately just giving him the soap and flannel (or a sponge is often better) should be the signal for him to wash himself and a tap on a limb he might have missed out be sufficient to remind him. Getting your face clean when you cannot see where it is dirty is not easy—if you do have to help do it as unobtrusively as possible, nothing destroys your pride at having managed something all by yourself than someone doing it all over again! Let him help to wash brothers (or sisters) and perhaps, in time, a washable doll.

Children sometimes develop fears about the noise of the water running out of the bath—if so, take child out of bath and bathroom before letting water run away. They soon grow out of phobias of this kind.

Daily washing hands and face at the basin before and after meals and after toiletting is no more a joyous occasion for the deaf/blind child than any other. It is an important habit to establish early and one you need to be both regular and firm about—once the initial display of dislike is over, this routine often becomes the first of the selfcare items to be achieved. It is in fact quite a complex sequence involving water, soap, towel, soaping, rinsing and drying. Always stand behind the child and to begin with dip his hands in the water and let him find the soap (which has already been put into the water) rub it on the backs and palms and then show him how to put it on the side of the basin. After rubbing his hands together, paddle them in the water and help him find the plug, pull it and feel the water going away until he can feel that the basin is quite empty. Drape the towel over his hands with a spare bit between them so that there is something to rub his hands together on. The natural extension of this routine is learning to turn the tap on and feeling the water coming out, finding the soap (where he has become used to putting it) and, when the washing is finished, finding the towel for himself. To wash his face drape the flannel over the upturned palms of his hands so that he can then bring it up to his face —squeezing the flannel for rinsing requires quite a lot of physical hand and wrist co-ordination and he will need help with this for quite a time.

Keep his toiletting things—towel, flannel and toothbrush, hairbrush and comb in a special place that is low enough for him to get without help.

The usual sequence for self-care in washing is:

Washes hands
Washes hands and dries
Washes and dries hands and face
Begins to wash himself in the bath
Brushes own hair (not efficiently of course)
Brushes own teeth
Can bath on own

Brushing teeth night and morning is very important. If at first a toothbrush is not tolerated you can try to wipe the teeth with a damp flannel with a little baking soda on it. However it is really better to find a very small soft brush and work up to a bigger, firmer one. Sometimes letting the child hold the brush with your help produces the response of opening the mouth.

Experiment with various flavours of toothpaste until you find one he seems to like helps—if he does not like a toothpaste, the smell of it

51

before it reaches his mouth will be enough to determine him not to open his mouth for the brush. An electric toothbrush may be the answer for some, particularly if they enjoy vibration.

Rubella children are often unlucky enough to have poor baby teeth which discolour quickly and wear down if they chew their toys a lot. The second teeth are usually good and remain so particularly if the child follows the common pattern of dislike for sweets. Regular visits to the dentist are a MUST, for toothache is very distressing for a child who is unable to tell you where the pain is and it is a pain which is very difficult to locate if you are not the actual sufferer.

Brushing and combing the hair is obviously part of this daily routine and again the child must be guided through the actions until he can take over on his own. Avoid making it a painful operation—remember he cannot see or be told how much nicer it is when it is done, nor can he know that everyone keeps their hair tidy—make sure he has a chance to feel the brush before you start so that he knows what it is you are going to do to him.

At all times give the appropriate communication sign for the activity and *Talk* to him about what is going on.

4. Feeding

As a social activity

Mealtimes are social occasions—within our own homes we may have differing standards, but outside there are broad standards to which we all conform. Since there will be occasions (many I hope) when your child will have meals outside his home, we must aim to achieve (in addition to self-feeding and eating normal foods) behaviour that will make such outings a pleasure to you both. In the course of learning to eat children go through stages which we discourage once they have served their purpose. With the feeding difficulties usually associated with deaf/blind children it may be necessary to deliberately encourage them to go through these early stages and it then becomes difficult to change them for the more grown up and acceptable ways of behaving at table. Finger feeding is one such stage. It is indeed valuable in giving awareness of textures of different foods and of the path which the food (and later the spoon) must take to the mouth. Some people advocate an initial period of eating anything and everything with the fingers, but I personally feel it should be confined to dry foods only, i.e. biscuits, bread, toast, fruit (pieces of apple, banana or orange sections) etc or such foods as can be cut into form small pieces, i.e. potato, meat, chicken, not in gravy. I would prefer to encourage the sense of smell for the kinds of food which should correctly be eaten with a spoon—he should be allowed to touch *all* new foods, but not eat them with his fingers if messy.

How much mess should we let him make at mealtimes? Some say

52

never mind the mess, but I feel it should not be more than is inevitable once a child begins to learn to feed himself. He can be made to feel the food he has chased off the plate onto the table as it happens and then shown how to replace it on spoon and plate immediately before taking another mouthful off the plate. He will have to learn this sometime, why not from the beginning as part of the regular routine.

I have already suggested that the child should join the family table at mealtimes in his highchair as soon as possible. Let him remain there until the family meal is finished. When he sits on an ordinary chair (of which he can generally get on his own) keep up this habit of waiting until the others have finished. There is nothing more distressing when you are out (or for the teacher at school) than a child who finished his meal before others and gets down and runs around—with a handicapped child it usually means the meal is ruined for everyone else. Allowing a book or small toy to hold, a hard biscuit to chew, or even to promise a sweet when everyone else is finished, is better for you and the child than a disrupted meal and frayed tempers. And you must be firm with the kind friend or relative who says "do let him get down"—if you are not consistent the child will never know what he is expected to do. If a child takes a long time to get through his meal, start him a little earlier, or see he gets his first. Give him only as much as you know he can manage in the normal time for that meal—long drawn out meals are frustrating for child and mother—if this cuts down the food intake give him an extra snack at bedtime.

Self-feeding

Make sure child is hungry if he opens his mouth when offered a spoonful he is hungry enough to feed himself!

It helps if you:

(a)   Gradually reduce the help you give, allowing the child to take over the last part of a sequence first as in previous routines.

(b)   Avoid surprising the child—i.e. don't leave him in the middle of a meal, or push the spoon into his mouth without giving him a chance to anticipate it, or put a new food or new utensil into his mouth without warning.

(c)   Remember mealtimes must be happy and not anxiety occasions.

(d)   Remember to learn about different foods you must be aware of them raw and cooked, whole and mashed, skinned and without skins.

(e)   Use plastic mug and plate—the latter can have a hot water compartment under for keeping the meal warm and is better with a good edge against which the child can push the spoon to load.

(f)   Remember children are very sensitive to temperature and test all hot foods before giving to the child—a burnt mouth can set feeding back weeks.

(g)   Go through the movements of self-feeding yourself so that you appreciate the sequence and can better keep it exactly the same each time.

(h)   Handedness—before you begin to teach him to feed himself, check which hand he uses most and put the spoon in that hand. It is important that he uses his dominant hand, once this has developed.

(i)   Use the sign for "eat" before each meal and the sign for "drink" before each drink.

(j)   The normal sequence for learning self-feeding is:
Eats with spoon
Eats with fork
Uses knife for spreading
Uses knife for cutting
Can manage own needs at table i.e. can help himself according to his requirements, does not need help with mashing, cutting, eating things like boiled egg, etc.

(k)   Watch for readiness for self-feeding i.e. he puts his hand on yours and helps you bring it to his mouth, has sufficient grasp to hold loaded spoon. It may be necessary to actually put his hand on yours to encourage this.

(l)   Thicken the handle of the spoon with foam rubber, plastic wood or sticky tape so that it is easier to grasp. Weight the spoon to increase hand control.

(m)   Children like different quantities at different ages—quantity does not increase to match size—will have periods when eats a lot and some when appetite is not so big.

(n)   Some children like to eat one thing before another, i.e. carrots, then meat, then potato.

Action sequence—stand behind chair

(a)   Put the spoon in the child's hand with yours over his, guide him through the action of scooping up the food, bringing it up towards the mouth until it is just inside the mouth, then let the child take the weight of the empty spoon and draw it out of his mouth on his own. Take his hand again and repeat process.

(b)   To begin with do this only for the first few mouthfuls, then finish the feed for him. Gradually increase the number of spoonfuls he is expected to help with until he does his bit throughout the course.

(c)   Take full spoon to just outside mouth, let him put it in and pull it out (repeat (b)).

(d)   Fill spoon—let child do rest on his own (repeat (b)).

(e)   Filling the spoon for himself required a complicated wrist movement—you might make him aware of the process by letting him

54

load the spoon by hand but avoid this becoming a habit, or he might be shown how to use a pusher. Practice of the wrist movement should be part of the skills he is learning in concurrent manipulative activities.

(f) A tap on the elbow should be enough to remind him to take the next mouthful once he is managing on his own.

(g) Scraping the food up when nearly at the end of the meal is also difficult and it is less frustrating for him if you devise an "all gone" sign and then remove the dish once it has all gone.

When first feeding himself it may be helpful to leave him on his own in a separate room so he can get on with the task without distraction, even from mummy.

Once your child can feed himself, try not to feed him any more (no matter how much it might save you time sometimes) because this is an area in which a child easily regresses in times of stress. If you give in you will soon find he learns to use as a lever to get your attention or his own way. If for any reason—illness or a hospital visit say—you do have to go back, at least go no further than helping him by guiding the spoon. Some children need this spoon guiding for a long time, but self-feeding is such an important milestone that we must be firm in keeping at the training.

Chewing

This is a key part of feeding for this is where the enjoyment of eating lies. It is common for these children not to chew. Chewing muscles are also speech muscles—use for one encourages use for the other. A child who does not chew but swallows his food in lumps is as likely to suffer from constipation as one who has too much liquidised food —constipation interferes with appetite and causes discomfort which will make the child unhappy—and an unhappy child learns nothing.

Biting bits of biscuit and other dry food is a necessary preliminary to chewing—hold small bits against his top teeth and gently push the lower jaw against until the piece is bitten off. Also let him put bits of biscuit into your mouth and feel you chewing—he needs to do this a lot in order to learn about the actions involved.

Drinking

Action sequence—child grasps cup or mug with two hands under yours, lifts from table, brings to lips, drinks and replaces on table. The last item is very important (particularly if cup is not empty)! and is the one you must expect the child to do by himself first. Let him take over movement by movement until he can manage the whole operation by himself. Give him the drink signal before you pick up the cup each time —he has achieved independence once when if given the drink sign, he

55

can carefully feel for the cup and take it up for himself without spilling. It helps if to begin with you put a little liquid in the cup so that if there is spilling, it doesn't swamp the child and upset him. Feeling for warmth is also an important clue, as is weight, but this latter develops only with experience.

Eating Normal Foods

Non-acceptance of a proper diet is a common problem, as is the inability to chew and obviously they are linked. If you cannot chew food to the state when it can be comfortably swallowed, then you are likely to reject lumpy foods. For this reason we have usually to go slowly through the sequence from milk/broth consistence to puree, sieved, minced, mashed and finally well chopped food. Familiar tastes may be preferred to new ones, you may get round this by introducing the new food slowly mixed with something he does like so long as it is of the same consistency, or by just giving one spoonful only at the beginning of a meal prior to familiar food and increasing the number of spoonfuls very slowly. Undoubtedly some of the feeding problems are due to a carry over of adult stress caused by worrying about the child not being properly nourished. These children tend to have poor appetites, to be small-built and eat less than most—but most of them manage normal foods in the end and do not seem to end up much smaller than their counterparts, so it is very much a matter of accepting this as a problem area and plodding on until it has been overcome. If progress has to be measured in terms of 2 spoonfuls this week, 4 next and 6 the next, thin last month, thicker this month, well you are making progress—keep a diary of this progress, it is usually very much more encouraging than looking at today's stage in isolation. Once a new item has been introduced or a new routine has been taken over, do not go back to the previous step.

Lap feeding may need to be continued while new textures are started, it is better to lap-feed one difficult meal than worry about the chair which offers none of the comfort that mum's arms and mum's voice have for what is an unpleasant, but necessary process for him. Expect him to be slow in the acceptance of new foods. He may cling to favourite foods for security. At the same time you are justified in expecting him to taste and try to eat new foods because the fact that YOU want it of him and his response being to please you, is an essential part of his growth. He is learning a human relationship, a response to a wish from another person, not his own wish—this is turning his attention outwards and is part of the whole educational process and basic to social training.

CHAPTER 8

MOTOR TRAINING

So far we have considered motor training in terms of the normal sequence of motor development. We have been encouraging our deaf /blind children in the activities that helped them go through the stages from lying to standing alone. We still have to complete these developmental sequences which are as follows:

1. *Walking*

    Sidesteps around playpen, walks around holding on to furniture, walks with both hands held, walks with one hand held, stands from lying by rolling onto tummy, kneeling and standing. Takes a few steps alone between two people, between furniture, walks alone freely. Can walk on tiptoe. Can walk backwards.

2. *Running*

    Runs stiffly has difficulty in stopping, runs with feet flat, can stop, runs pulling and pushing toys, runs lightly on toes.

3. *Jumping*

    Likes to be jumped up and down two hands held—makes attempt to jump own body, can jump alone, can jump off step, can jump over small object on floor, jumps over a low string.

4. *Stairs*

    Crawls upstairs, creeps down backwards, walks up and down stairs holding onto rail two feet to each step, walks up alone and down holding on still two feet per step. Walks up alone alternating feet on stair, walks up and down alternating feet.

5. *Moving with an object*

    Pushes, pulls and carries large toys, pulls toy with cord, throws small ball without falling, walks into large ball if tries to kick it. Steers large toys, rides a tricycle.

These sequences take us up to the normal 5 year old developmental stage, but timing is not important for the deaf/blind child—what is important is that you should be aware of the sequence so that you will know the next step to prepare him for as each item is achieved. It also provides you with information to pass on to the teacher when your child joins a preschool group so that you can plan together the means of completing the remaining steps.

Important to all the above are body image, balance, rhythm, gait, posture and co-ordination of body parts. Let's look briefly at some of the ways we can help to develop these things and so improve the quality of movement.

Body Image

Rolling over and over (clothed and unclothed) on a hard surface so that he is aware of body parts as they meet the surface. (Also on grass, pattern lino).

Sitting in a large cardboard box lined with as many different surfaces as you can find, with as little clothing as possible so he can feel the varying textures with the whole of his body.

Placing toys in his clothing so that he can retrieve them from all sorts of awkward places.

Crawling under things (mummy, the table) through things (hoop) between things (2 cardboard boxes) over things (cushion roll, pile of cushions).

Getting into and out of things (cardboard box, armchair).

Little sandbags on wrists or ankles to make aware of lifting hands and feet.

Crawl under rope or stick without touching with body.

Step over rope without touching it.

Make a little obstacle course so he has to do several of the above in a sequence.

Balance

Holding child in your arms let him feel you turn, go up and down, change speed etc.

Sit him on your lap (a) facing you both hands held or (b) back to you held by one hand, and wobble him about. With you lying on your back, sit child on your knees and holding both his hands let him do up and down or wobble about—reduce the firmness of your hold as his confidence grows.

Let him experience all kinds of activity with you—use you as a climbing frame, have rides on your back (you on all fours), give him piggybacks, shoulder rides etc.

Walkride him on your feet (his back to you). Sometimes let his balance depend on each leg in turn.

You sit and let him stand on your knees—hold his hands (later his hips) and wobble your legs.

(In all the above put him off balance just enough to give him a tinge of insecurity, but not enough to make him frightened).

Rhythm

Awareness of rhythm through you as you hold him and sway, dance or stamp, rock him on your knees to music.

58

Actions to nursery songs with you and later on own.
Feeling rhythm through a vibrating surface (whole body if possible).
Beating rhythms on drum.
Awareness of outside rhythm helps to develop the individual inner rhythm which is essential to easy and co-ordinated movements.

Gait

When he can walk freely a deaf/blind child may need to be taught to control his gait and stride so that he does not go lunging forward or falling behind because his stride is too big or too small. Training to walk through rungs of a ladder placed on the floor, in and out of shallow boxes placed at appropriate stride length or, if vision permits, on footprints or coloured squares taped to the floor.

Posture

There is a great tendency for these children to walk with head bent forward too much or, if tied to light sources, to tilt their heads back. A moving light at the child's eye level will encourage travel and keep the head erect and facing forward.

Co-ordination of Body Parts

To walk properly not only requires child to be able to synchronize the movements of his legs, but also to co-ordinate the swing of his arms —to encourage this you must fit your stride to that of your child when you are walking hand in hand and move his hand to swing appropriately to the foot placement. When this can be managed on flat ground, slopes up and down should be taught.

So far we have been concerned with activities for moving in space —moving on things i.e. swinging, sliding, rocking, are also enjoyed —some vital to mobility others giving pleasure in release of energy and others as activities shared with you, all giving him awareness of what his body can do and what he can do with his body. In addition there are activities which we do with our hands, our arms and our legs and they can be taught by getting the child to do them with us until he can take over and do them by himself. What is important here is that we should provide a reason for the activity being taught that is interesting enough for him to want to do it for himself. The following are some suggestions, but I am sure that you will quickly get the basic idea and then find lots of other ways of helping to practice and perfect these skills. The child must frequently and repeatedly be shown how to do them. He must experiment with different objects (i.e. throw a big ball, a small ball, woolly, heavy, light balls etc). He must have freedom to do it by himself when he is ready. Confidence comes from being well practiced in the skill and being allowed to go on his own at the right moment i.e. while he is still keen and not bored by doing it too often.

Fine Hand Skills
One Hand
  Picking up small objects—smarties or $\frac{1}{4}$ chocolate drops
  Carrying small objects—taking a smartie to mummy
  Squeezing—squeaky toy for noise or puff of air
  Twisting—nuts and bolts plastic toy
  Turning—music box with handle tap to get water
  Screwing—paper spills to thread through hole
  Poking—to burst soap bubbles

Two Hands
  Tearing—paper (because it's fun and normal)
  Turning—wheels on car (pedal)
  Banging—on a drum or old guitar with strings removed
  Pulling apart—dough or plasticine or large lego
  Pushing together—dough or plasticine or large lego

Big Arm Movements
  Reaching—for things he wants
  Waving arms—to music
  Clapping—to music, nursery rhymes
  Hitting—ball, balloon
  Hugging—loving
  Patting—loving
  Picking up large objects—stacking cushions, boxes
  Picking up heavy objects—bucket of sand, box of bricks
  Pushing—pram, trolley
  Pulling—musical pullalong toys
  Throwing, catching—various sized balls

Directed Movements
  Things in hand/s towards one—hat on head
  Using tools—spoonful of food to mouth, hammering toys
  Objects from one place to another—picking up fallen toy and putting on table, in box etc

Leg Movements
  Kicking—balls
  Riding a tricycle
  Riding a scooter

I have quite deliberately given you lists in this chapter as opposed to a training programme. Where motor training is concerned only *you* must be conscious that a particular skill is being deliberately encouraged. For the child it must ALWAYS be the fun of the total activity and part of every day living. The lists have not been set out in any developmental order nor are the items in each list in order of difficulty. It is up to you to be aware of the importance of these skills and provide opportunities for them to be practiced.

Motor skills are essential to play and social activities—the daily occurrence of play and social activities provides opportunity to learn and improve motor skills. We cannot find out about our world without movement of ourselves or part of ourselves towards, away from over, around the objects in it or without movements which enable us to manipulate these objects. We cannot indeed communicate with one another without movement, for speech, finger spelling and signing are movement.

Movement is essential to our way of living—as their motor development progresses and opportunity arises, there is no reason at all why deaf/blind children should not enjoy all the activities I have mentioned just as most other children do at some time in their childhood.

CHAPTER 9
MOBILITY

Mobility is the ability to find our way around independently, doing so because we want to or because we have a reason to move. Curiosity about things he sees and hears first prompts a child to begin to move about. As his experiences widen and he becomes physically more able, he moves confidently and purposefully in an ever increasing number of environments, i.e. his home, other homes, his school, the shops, other towns etc etc. Without visual and auditory clues the deaf /blind child has little to entice him to move, nor is it easy for him to learn of reasons why he should move. It is true that he is often attracted to light and will move to a source of light and this is a useful tool for training movement skills, but too often it distracts his attention from the valuable clues that aid mobility.

Every activity of the child before he becomes mobile prepares him for mobility, because to move about a child must be not only physically able, but must be aware of objects in his surroundings and his relationship with them. At first the deaf/blind baby's world is no more than half a circle—his awareness of what is around him goes no further than the stretch of his arms outwards and upwards. So long as he lies on his back it cannot go any further, that is why it is so important that he learns to sit up (even if only propped up) at the right age. When he sits his world is still a semi circle until he learns to balance and twist round to reach behind him, but far more experiences can be brought to within this area than when he is lying. Once he can crawl his world extends in terms of floor space and in the number of objects he can now encounter for himself such as toys, people's feet, furniture, steps etc. When he stands upright, he takes in a whole new world of experiences and has to learn about things from a new level—i.e. whereas before he could only move under a table, he can now also walk round it. We have to help him learn as much as possible about the things in his environment before he goes by himself—how they differ in size, texture, colour, shape, temperature, weight, movement, and sound (see Chapter on Learning). He has to know about things in a way that makes them meaningful, that is they must be real things, a bed is to lie on, you can walk round it, go under it, it has corners, is soft etc, a spoon is to eat with, you can have big or small ones, scoop or dig with them, fill and empty them, a chair is to sit on, a door is there to be opened and shut (not slammed!). If an object is one which could be used for a number of purposes the deaf/blind child needs to be taught only its main purpose at this stage—a bed is a place to lie on and go to sleep, it's not a place for playing with toys, getting dressed on etc, it is a reference point for moving about the bedroom only if it is associated with a recognised activity.

To learn about the objects around him in such a way that they are recognisable to him means making use of his intact and residual senses, that is use as much sight and hearing as he possesses, together with touch, feeling, smell and movement. To make full use of tactile clues we must supplement touch by the hand with tactile information from other parts of the body, such as bare feet for awareness of say the carpet in one room and lino in the kitchen. Some deaf/blind children do not like touching things and it may be necessary to physically move the child's body over, through and around the objects. Coverings of various textures, some of which can be deliberately placed within reach along his pathway, such as smooth and rough, scratchy and bobbly all add to the quality of the information being gathered. Where vision can help a mirror may provide a clue, a colour or texture differing rail for each room, or small carved wood panel by the door at hand height appropriately clued can aid mobility and help to provide the sense of security which is very important when this training is in its first stages. The sense of smell is secondary to the other senses, but is nevertheless useful, a bowl of oranges identified by shape and texture is confirmed by its distinct smell.

What we are concerned with is to make it easy and interesting for a child to get about—so that he wants and is able to do so on his own.

To be mobile a child must possess:

1. The ability to distinguish himself from his environment, that is he must be aware that he has a hand so that he can distinguish between his hand and what he is holding or touching, only then can the object be meaningfully explored.
2. The ability to walk alone or at least walk with one hand held.
3. An awareness of things that are stationary—the door, wall, bath, stairs etc, because such things give him clues as to the direction in which other things are to be found, i.e. the light switch is on the right of the door.
4. An awareness of objects which are moveable—things which will not always be found in the same place, i.e. chairs, toys, etc.
5. An awareness of objects which he may find moving—people, animals, cars, the hoover etc.
6. Recognition of these things as things he has had contact with before and of their position in the pathway along which he is travelling.

63

Of course our deaf/blind child will move about with or without help, but unless we teach him to move about for a purpose he is likely to develop the habit of aimless movement from one place to another and what is more, come to resent being required to move from one place to another when this is necessary. Of course he will move freely according to his own need when at play, but during the day there are regular daily activities which provide the training ground for mobility of which we must take advantage now if our child is to be fully and independently mobile later on.

You can think of mobility as a series of circles each bigger than the previous one. Learning about the room he plays in is the first circle, the house is the next, then the garden round the house, the streets and so on. IT BEGINS IN HIS OWN HOME. A sample sequence might be as follows:

A. Sitting Room—To go round the outside of the room.
    Teach him to go from the door to the table to have a meal.
    Teach him to go from the door to his toybox to play.
    Teach him to go from his toybox to mummy's chair/daddy's chair for a romp etc.
    Teach him to go from the above back to the door.
B. From A to the kitchen where he could learn the way round the kitchen to the cupboard for a mug, to the fridge for some milk or orange juice and to the larder for a biscuit.
C. From A and from B up the stairs to round the bathroom and/or toilet—to locate the toilet, bath, basin and washing things.
D. From C to go round the bedroom, to get into bed or to places where clothes are kept.
E. From D and C down the stairs to any of the previously learned routes to the various rooms or to where his coat and hat are kept and from there to the front door if going for a walk or to the door to the garden if going to play outside.

In all cases *teach* the route back, because here the recognised objects appear in the reverse order. You teach him by walking behind him with one hand held by you to indicate the direction you want him to go, his other hand you hold over its back so that you can guide it over the reference point on route. You take exactly the same route every time and stop to feel each reference point. Ultimately when he goes on his own he will need to give no more than a cursory touch to alert him to where he is and the direction he needs to follow. Start him off when you think he is ready to try alone, on the straight bits—i.e. trailing his hand along a wall, feeling it a little ahead of his body. When he can manage the straight bit he must be shown how to get across or through openings —if door is not too wide he can locate the opposite side to begin with by stretching the other hand across the space, later he will know to continue to take several steps in the same direction as he is going. He must be able to do this before he is allowed to go alone across larger breaks. If he needs to turn a corner, his hand follows the turn then his body follows.

If he wants to get to something in the room the "squaring off" technique is useful. To get to table in the centre of the room—child steps into room, puts back against wall next to door, then walks forward to the table (the position of which he is aware).

Guiding a child along the desired route by getting him to follow a bright light or a sound source (bell, voice etc) may be helpful when he is gaining confidence to move into space on his own.

If you notice your child putting out his arms for protection or to locate a wall, encourage him, in preference, to bring one arm up and straight forward at shoulder level, bending his arm at the elbow across his body towards the other shoulder. This gives better protection from bumps for the upper part of the body than just extending the arms which protects only a narrow part of the body's width. For the protection of the lower part of the body show the child how to let one arm hang straight at his side, then keeping it straight move it across the body towards the opposite hip.

To begin with you may need to arrange furniture in such a way that it provides reference points at suitable intervals and have some guide (cord) across a wide gap. The toybox needs to be in a place easily located. If your child is tempted to use an easier method of travelling (crawling) discourage this at the times you are actually carrying out mobility training.

Not only are we teaching the deaf/blind child how to make use of his environment to get around, to recognise places for what occurs in them, but when he leads us along these routes or goes by himself he is telling us—communicating—his need for what goes on there. How marvellous when he finds his way to the larder because he is hungry! It is absolutely vital that we respond immediately by giving him or doing for him what he wants so that he knows we have understood him. At the same time we must beware of 'finding the way to the larder for a biscuit' becoming a too frequent habit and have something handy to distract him, or reward him only when he has come via the reference points for this is what we are trying to teach—the need to use objects in the environment to enable him to move about without sight and sound clues.

Always talk to your child about the things he touches and the route he is taking. If your communication system is one of signing you must still talk, but in addition give the appropriate sign when you begin the route and when the goal is reached—drink, toys, daddy, bed etc. During actual mobility training it may be less confusing if you do not sign the names of the objects which are reference points (at all other times yes), rather would I sign pleasure at his progress.

Safety. Deaf/blind children will have falls as will all children, perhaps a few more due to lack of sight and not hearing the warning voice. A sign to convey the concept of "take care" would be valuable when the child is beginning to follow routes for himself, perhaps a tap on the front of the shoulder. They must be allowed to face the same dangers as normal children if they are to function independently, but until communication is well established the following seem to me to be vital precautions:

A guard round the fire
A gate at the top of the stairs or at bedroom door at night
No table cloths which can pull off
Kitchen liquids and medicines in locked cupboard, key out of reach

These same techniques should be used for each of the environments he moves out into as he gets older. Finding his way out of doors along streets, on transport, etc on his own comes very much later and should be learned with the help of mobility officer of the Blind Welfare Service. In the meantime you will be his guide along these routes—taking him by the hand whilst he is little but when he gets tall enough, encourage him to grasp your arm just above the elbow because he can gain many cues to travel through this contact with you. Keep your arm close to your body so that the child is kept close to you and will get the feeling of the movements you make as signals as to what he must do. Stay about a half pace ahead of the child so he receives the signals before having to actually make the movements. Initially walk at the child's pace, stopping and starting slowly and easily—do not push, pull or shove the child and never leave alone without physical (or visual) contact with the environment (i.e. hand on wall etc if you need to use both your hands to open a lift door, find your keys and open the front door, or hand on car whilst you get doors unlocked). Negotiate turns at a wide angle, particularly a right turn, so that you do not get across his path as you turn.

Going down stairs you must stop at first step and allow child to locate the step edge with his foot, then move down, keeping one step ahead of the child who will know when the bottom has been reached because your movements continue forward not down.

When the way is narrow, give a movement of your arm towards midline of your back as signal for child to move behind you, preferably straightening his arm to keep distance between you and avoid him kicking your heels. Bringing your arm to normal position will signal child to come back to your side.

Mobility is important to emotional development. It is all too easy to *take* your child everywhere, so that he comes to expect this and never develops any desire to go alone. We ourselves need to become "reference points" from which our child can begin to move away and from whom he will need less and less clues as he becomes more and more confident. It is natural to want to do things for him, but, unless we are careful, by doing too much for him for too long, we strengthen the bonds between us, bonds which must be broken to achieve independence, broken by mobility.

CHAPTER 10
EMOTIONAL DEVELOPMENT

Emotions are both complex and individual. The word "emotion" means feeling and emotional development includes our own personal feelings, the way we feel about ourselves, towards others and the way that others feel towards us. We hope that children will grow up emotionally stable and this means they will have learned to cope with their own feelings and the way others feel towards them, whether these feelings are pleasant or unpleasant, without getting unduly upset.

Individual emotions develop in each of us in a certain sequence—as is to be expected if you think about it. You have to feel love before you can feel that which is not love (dislike, hate), to feel trust before you can distrust, to enjoy something before you feel anger when it is taken away from you, to feel frustration before having a temper tantrum, to be aware of familiar things to fear them when they appear in an unfamiliar guise. The very young baby will when awake be either generally totally excited or distressed (as when hungry); at six months he will show friendliness to all people, displeasure at the removal of a toy; at nine months he shows fear of strangers, by one year he shows affection for family and anxiety if a familiar adult is not present. In another six months he alternates between wanting to be independent yet still needing to cling. By 2 he treats other children with affection, but will also show jealousy if they get more attention than he does. By $2\frac{1}{2}$ he is usually active, restless and rebellious and this is when he begins to feel frustrated and show his temper. By the time he is 5 he is learning to be more restrained because he has observed this in those around him, has been praised when he has shown restraint and because he has an understanding of time to come (wait a minute) and so he is able to accept some denial and some frustration.

This sequence is naturally linked with the various stages of development in other areas. The deaf/blind child is at a distinct disadvantage for emotional growth unless we have provided for growth in these other areas too. Before he can be friendly or fear strangers he must know he is a person himself, that he is like others, but that there are also differences between others that determine whether you behave in a friendly manner or fear them ... indifference to others is frequently seen in deaf/blind children and without a relationship with another person he has no means of receiving information, so we have a vicious circle. A deaf/blind child must have experienced pleasure in something and remember this before he can feel a need for it, and must know about communicating, before he can get frustrated at not being able to get you to understand what he wants. In other words, although he should have the capacity to develop these emotions, certain experiences are necessary in order to use them. These experiences are also only within the capacity of a child at a certain stage of development, so emotions develop sequentially and are related to experience and learning. If you have so few experiences that you have learned neither to do or not to do, you will never get frustrated.

Awareness of the love of his parents allows a child to move away from them to explore, but whilst he is gaining confidence he frequently returns to your side to reassure himself. Mother is the centre of a widening circle, it is knowing she is there always loving, that is important to every child including the deaf/blind. He does not, however, necessarily know that you are within reach (except when he is on your lap or being led by hand) and so it is very much up to us to give him this awareness of our presence by frequently going to him, touching him, talking to him, picking him up, playing with him for a few minutes. Have him playing in the room in which you are working and when you sit down to remain in a room, have him play close to your feet. A sense of love and security is an essential preliminary to all other emotional development. There is, however, a more important aspect of emotional development. The opposite to the emotionally stable personality is one who is described as emotionally disturbed. The person who cannot control his emotions, who does things which draw attention to himself, perhaps to make people think he is the person he would like to be but is sure he is not, who is irresponsible and does not care about others, who is unable to make relationships with others and is withdrawn, who fails to make a go of things and eventually gives up trying, who is over anxious and lacks confidence in himself. It is believed that this kind of emotional disturbance is a result of certain inborn needs of the young child not being met. Just as there is a need to communicate born in every child, so each is also believed to feel a need for:

Love and security
Stimulating experiences
Achievement
Personal independence

Parents are the first in line to meet these needs, yet they are the people who at such a time themselves feel insecure, whose own emotions may well have been upset by having a handicapped child, for whom the responsibility of bringing up a handicapped child is a heavy one and one they doubt they will do successfully. It is quite natural to feel like this, but you have to try not to let these feelings overwhelm you for it is possible that in understanding and providing for your child's emotional needs, you will iron out some of your own difficulties.

Let us look at emotional needs in more detail.

1. A child needs to be loved and cared for in such a way that he knows he is important to you whatever he may be like or whatever he may do. If he senses disapproval he will become anxious and anxiety, because it is such an unpleasant feeling, makes a child restless and unable to cope with the demands made upon him in other ways, i.e. feeding, toiletting etc. He must experience love before he can give it and already we have talked about making a good relationship with mother in the first months as a necessary preliminary to relationships with others. Loving him this way does not mean letting him have and do just what he likes, he like any other child must be disciplined when it is necessary, but not in such a way that he feels we no longer love him. He must know for certain that despite all the difficulties and anxieties he will undoubtedly cause us, we love him.

2. Right from the day we are born new things are happening to us, we learn and do something new every day, we add new experiences to those we have already and we are doing this all our lives. We have a need to be stimulated in this way, it keeps us lively, interested and interesting. Deaf/blind children when they are very young cannot receive much stimulation unless deliberately given them, and stimulation through the tactile sense not backed by sight and hearing, is not so easily meaningful that it encourages the child to seek more and more new experiences. The incentive to seek experience loses its impetus quickly in many of these children and we are often faced not only with difficulty of putting things across to him, but also faced with a child who lacks within himself the incentive for external stimulation and turns to self-stimulation and withdraws from contact with people (even you his parents), cutting at source the opportunity for emotional development.

3. Achievement is important to all of us—failure creates anxiety and a feeling of inferiority. It is up to us to see that the handicapped child is provided with opportunities that stretch his abilities to the full, but allow him success. He should not be expected to compete with normal children for this is setting our sights too high. Nor, on the other hand, must we set them too low—we must be prepared to adjust as time goes by and match our aims with the

child's abilities as they develop. Having said the above, it does not mean that a deaf/blind child must never experience failure, he will have to learn to cope with difficulties, but we must see that these are not so great as to discourage him from trying to overcome them. He will need your praise not only for what he achieves, but for good effort and you must show him that you accept that some mistakes are all part and parcel of the process of learning.

4. Personal independence. This is really much more than being able to do things for himself, although this is where it begins. Like the 18 months child who alternates between feeling he wants to have a go by himself, yet loves mummy to go on doing things for him still, so will the deaf/blind child tend to let us go on doing things unless we watch out for those little signs of effort on his part and encourage him then to do it himself. He will almost certainly refuse to make an effort himself if what we ask is difficult and this is why we must be so careful about breaking down into the sort of small steps he will best manage one at a time. Whenever he shows he wants to try something himself let him—even sometimes if this may seem risky, for independence is born of knowing how to cope with your environment, without a chance to try, he never will learn. Whilst we cannot expect complete independence, every little thing that our child can do for himself and by himself, will strengthen his self-respect and make him a happier person. Independence is not complete without the sense of responsibility which grows from not only being able to help himself, but to help others. So when the time comes for us to begin allowing him to lay the table, carry a plate to the table, wash up, dust etc, even if it may mean something gets broken (they should only be old things whilst he is becoming proficient) we must do so for it all adds to his stature as a person.

Special Problems

Temper tantrums in the deaf/blind child should to some extent be regarded as a positive sign. If he expresses frustration he must be aware of something to get frustrated over. When such behaviour includes aggression he is demonstrating an important emotional constituent of all of us because it is one that helps us overcome difficulties. The screaming kicking child is showing an energy source which needs to be used in more acceptable ways to help him reach satisfying goals. We therefore need to guard against controlling aggression too sharply, particularly by a show of aggression in retaliation. This is not easy, particularly when he chooses to have a temper tantrum in public. Nor must we control it by giving in, for this just gives him licence to repeat the tantrum whenever he cannot get his own way. The best method of dealing with a temper tantrum is first to observe what causes it. If it is lack of communication do your best to find out what he was trying to "say" and then teach him the sign. If it occurs because he wants to do or have something that is not possible, then make sure you avoid repetition in future by removing the toy (or whatever) and provide a substitute which he can have. Remember a temper tantrum is not a nice experience and a child is often frightened when he loses control of himself in this way. When he is small it is best to hold him very very firmly and lovingly until he relaxes. It is not so easy with the older child, but if it is necessary to restrain him, then this is best done by standing behind him holding his hands, his arms having been crossed in front of him. They need comforting when it is over and if they appear exhausted give a warm sweet drink or a short rest. This must not appear as a reward or it is likely to increase the very behaviour we want to discourage.

One frequent cause of temper tantrums is the child not being given consistent guidelines to what he may or may not do. If one day you are too busy to take away a valued object and he is allowed to play with it, can you blame him for being confused and upset if the next day you have time to say no and stop him! Being cross with him for something one day and allowing it the next because he makes a fuss shows him there is one way to get what he wants and he will try it out whenever he has a chance.

Relationship

A child who cannot make a relationship is often inert and motiveless, unresponsive to incentive of praise, encouragement or reward. Equally so if you his mother get little response to your attempts to make a relationship with your child, it is easy to feel discouraged and start responding in a mechanical way. Once you cease to relate to him, he has no hope of learning how to relate himself. It often takes a long time for these children to relate to anyone and you must be prepared for this—it will come and must come before he can develop as a person himself.

Chapter 11

PLAY AND LEARNING—PART 1

Early Play Experiences

When we use the word "play" it is usually to describe the activities of a young child's life that are not directly concerned with daily routines. So far as the deaf/blind child is concerned we have already mentioned play between ourselves and the child in the form of "games" that will provide the early communication and movement experiences. What we are thinking about now is play with toys with which a normal child would occupy himself without much intervention from adults and from which he would be learning about things in his world and with which he would be practicing the skills needed for living in that world.

If you observe a young baby when he first plays with toys he holds them, shakes and bangs them, waves them about, looks at them and listens to the noises they make. At first he can hold only one toy and if given two has to drop one—when he can hold two he rubs or bangs them together. He repeats these actions over and over again just for the pleasure repeating them gives him. When he can sit up he adds throwing, knocking down and dropping toys to his repertoire, watching where they fall, the noise they make when they drop and he will do this as often as we are willing to pick them up for him. In the next stage he explores his toys and play is for learning. He examines his toys for their detail, for their use and for what he can do with them —some fit inside each other, some come to pieces if you take parts off or pull them apart, some make a noise and so on. After a period of this kind of play he begins to experiment with toys, using them in different ways, putting them together in different ways, filling them, emptying them, carrying, pushing and pulling them about and generally discovering the effect of his own actions. These three stages of play—actions, exploring and doing—occur before play of the kind through which a child learns about such things as similarities, differences, relationships between things—i.e. sorting, matching, sets—and becomes involved in fine motor skills, all of which you will find in detail in Part 2 of this chapter.

It is important to remember that this sequence of play in the normal child does not happen in isolation—the potential is there, but it is through his relationship with us, *our* participation in and verbal comment on his play, that development is encouraged. Nor are the divisions I have drawn clear cut, they overlap, and each is necessary to the development of certain emerging skills such as focussing the eyes, hand-eye co-ordination, judging distance and depth, recognising shape, colour, texture, size. All these things we are reinforcing as we talk to him—look at this, put it on here, it's fallen on the floor, Mummy pick it up, here it is, it's red, like a ball, round and soft and so on.

Play of this kind and in the above sequence is just as important for the deaf/blind child as for any other. But we shall have to teach him how to play. Of course once he has learned to play he will need opportunity to repeat it on his own and in various ways. At all times we must encourage him to feel things so that not only does he become familiar with all aspects of a toy, but in time will only need to become aware of one or two of these in order to be able to recall the whole and its associated uses. This skill is so vital to all his future, learning begins here and we must have it in mind always.

If we have played with our child as suggested in the earlier chapters, we shall by now have a very good idea of whether he has enough useful vision to be attracted by bright colours and if so this is our best means of engaging his attention to new toys and his interest in their exploration and use. If the sight is poor, but there is interest in sounds, we must choose toys with a good auditory component. If we have had difficulty in getting our child even to hold toys and he just drops or pushes them away, we shall need to use quite a different approach before moving to stages 1, 2 and 3.

The toys our deaf/blind child needs in stage 1 are:

> Brightly coloured or shiny—rattles, bell toys, squeakers, musical box.
>
> Small woolly toys, balls, or soft toys covered in different soft materials, with bell inside for hanging where he can touch or kick them or for holding.
>
> Box of baby shapes.
>
> Balloons, mobiles for shape and colour, or mobiles which tinkle.
>
> Pram toys—strung across where he can touch them with his hands or feet, accidentally as well as deliberately.

If he does not play spontaneously we must teach him by holding his hands round these toys, showing him how to shake and bang them and when he does do this of his own accord, encouraging him to reach for them by holding them just out of his reach, just touching him with them and moving slightly so that there is a reaching out or feeling around for them. Give him one at a time, allowing him to get used to it by putting it frequently into his hand and activating it with him. Once he has begun to play with one toy you can give him others that are similar and allow some play with the one type of toy before introducing another kind, then treat the new one in the same way at the same time allowing some periods of play with the toys handled previously, so building up to a variety of toys gradually. This play occurs at about the same time as your child begins to hold some of the things that are used in daily routines—the hair brush, tooth brush, cup, spoon, shoe. You must expect and allow your child to mouth and smell toys and to do this a lot longer than the normal child for the tongue, lips and nose of a blind child provide valuable clues that must not be denied him. Of course we do have to be on our guard that this is not the *only* thing that our child does with toys.

Talk and laugh with your child when you play with him with his toys and when he is willing to take them from you and bang them etc, you must encourage him to give them back to you. Play peepboo—a paper hankie over his face for him to pull off, and over your face for him to pull off too. Show him how to hide things and find them.

There is a natural progression (about the time he sits well alone) from this kind of action play to the exploratory kind as a child's perceptual awareness increases. The deaf/blind child, however, may stick at stage 1 and not move on unless we initiate him into exploratory play. We must notice if he is quickly tired of his banging toys, or goes on doing the same thing with the same toy for long periods, or just gets bored and reverts to hand-flapping, eye-poking or any form of self stimulation. If so you must make time to sit him on your lap and play with the following things:

Wind-up toys—feel the key going round, the toy in action, listen to the noise it makes, feel the vibration.

Balls—box of balls, one each large, small, soft, hard, rubber, plastic, with bell in, rough surface (or pattern on), plastic with holes in etc. With your hands over the child's show him how to throw up, put in and out of box, bag or other suitable container.

Drum, wrist bells, hand bells, clackers, squeaker toys—noise making toys that he can bang on or operate with his hands.

Small tins—instant coffee size well sealed, with rice, pebbles, paper clips, salt etc inside for shaking. (Can also make shakers with yoghurt cartons, washing up liquid bottles etc).

Nesting cups, eggs or other toys that fit inside each other.

Rings or balls on sticks.

Large plastic beads or bricks that can be pulled apart.

(These last three items require at this stage to be taken apart i.e. balls *off* stick but not put on yet, nesting cups taken out, or down from pile, *not* built up).

When you leave him to play on the floor with any of these things by himself it is a good idea sometimes to give them to him in a large plastic transparent box and to have another box which is empty, so that as he takes the things out one by one, he can put them into the other box. (He will need showing how to do this and perhaps reminding, but it is better than always having them all over the place and having difficulty in finding them). Having a basket, or big cardboard box to keep all his toys in follows on from this training, so that he can get toys for himself knowing they will always be found in the one place, and so that you can teach him at the end of play time to put away his toys—both very important items in the process of learning to play.

When the deaf/blind child begins to put together some of the things he previously only took apart, and he is able to move about on hands and knees or walk alone, we shall know he is beginning to move into stage 3. He will use many of the toys from stage 2, but in different ways, particularly building them up. He will play with water or sand and enjoy filling his nesting cups etc with them, he will need all sorts of things like cotton reels, pebbles, (large enough not to be swallowed), bottle tops, plastic offcuts—anything that is suitable to be handled and carried around in containers. You will find he will enjoy a "bit box" (with one each of a variety of tin lids, small boxes, spools—small objects of different shapes, colours and sizes).

Other suggestions are:

Clothespegs round a tin—to take off and put on.

Two toys lightly fastened together by cellotape to be pulled apart.

A fair-sized doll with easily removed clothes—he will probably start with removing its hat and shoes.

A familiar (or new) toy in a parcel for him to unwrap.

Several little sealed material bags containing stones, dried beans, salt, feathers etc to be tossed, hidden, found etc.

A hand mirror, comb and hairbrush, old blanket and little pillow.

Old magazines—to tear, crush, fold etc.

Pull along toys, trucks or toy prams to put toys in and push around.

Sand and water.

Balls—now to be used in play with another person.

There is little doubt that a deaf/blind child will always need help in all new play situations and I think that what you show him must be the traditional way of play with the material—he may imitate this, he may find other ways for himself. All experimentation is good—over-repetition is a sign that he needs to have a new toy and to be shown how to play with it.

The deaf/blind child needs to have all these play experiences, but he must not be rushed through them. He has very limited channels through which to receive the information play provides, therefore the toys are not so inviting or stimulating enough to keep his interest for long periods. It is a good idea to keep play periods very short and intersperse them with a movement activity—say a few minutes on a swing (indoor and outdoor) or in a rocking chair, the walkie pen, learning about what you are doing, or one of the motor games—so that he has toys for frequent short periods rather than one long period.

If as a result of you spending time teaching your child to play he eventually enjoys play and playthings enough to develop the ability to play constructively by himself, then every minute will have been worthwhile. A child who cannot occupy himself in play is unlikely to be able later on to occupy himself in learning and will fall back on continuous repetitive twiddling of favourite objects—this leads to boredom, frustration, temper tantrums with no alternative to relieve these feelings but return to the twiddling. Twiddling is a meaningful sensory motor activity in the baby, but it is sad to see it in the older child and sometimes still in the adult.

Let us return to the deaf/blind child who shows absolutely no interest in toys beyond holding them momentarily up to his eyes and then just drops them, despite all our efforts to show him how to play. Such a child is not being attracted by what is new as is usually the case and so we have to start him off with familiar things—or rather familiar things but an altered version—that are connected with the satisfaction of his daily needs, things he cannot afford not to be aware of. During feeding a spoon acquires significance—a spoon of an unusual shape may well surprise him into exploring it which will be so with a bottle if he is bottle fed, brush and comb, shoe, and so on. It is hoped that gradually the images built up from this kind of play will become separated from the original activity and the interest in them as playthings extend to the play sequences described above, although it will be a lot later, perhaps years, than the deaf/blind child who is willing to handle toys from the first. Playing with you may first also need encouraging by you joining in his stereotype activities, i.e. hand-flapping, finger-play, spinning things, letting him feel you copying his actions and then you altering these so that he has experience of different actions he can also do.

Points to remember

Always try to find simple things which your child can use successfully before giving him more complicated toys.

Early toys need to be easily washed as they will be explored by mouth. Attach toys to cot, table or playpen but make sure your child knows that they are attached—let him feel the tape or string right up to the end and then to the toy.

Close your eyes and try handling the toys yourself—it helps you to choose those most likely to give him enjoyment.

Make sure paint and pigments are non-poisonous and that soft toys do not have eyes etc, that are fastened with wire and can work loose.

Over and above the joy play provides, children get pleasure from improving their skills and play that absorbs a child sets the pattern for his approach to tasks in the future.

A child learns by doing and he learns only as much as he does.

Knowledge grows by taking things apart and putting them together in new inventions—give him things that ask to be pulled apart and show him ways of re-arranging them, then let him have a go. New learning uses and builds upon previous learning—this means a carefully planned sequence of small steps is as essential in play as in other areas of development.

The unoccupied baby, "good" though he may seem to be, is one who needs most help.

These are the years when most time needs to be spent with your deaf /blind baby—if it means leaving the chores sometimes or having some help in the home (and financial aid is available from several sources nowadays) it is more than worthwhile.

PLAY AND LEARNING—PART 2

Parents and teachers—Informal and Formal Programmes

The fourth phase of play and learning, to which we now come, is by far the most complex. It is the period when, through play, exploration, manipulation and interaction with adults and their peers children learn the skills which prepare them for the activities they will do when they go to school. So far as deaf/blind children are concerned, programmes to provide the learning experiences relative to this preschool period, have not usually been presented to them until entering school at the age of 5 or even later. This has been necessary because there has been very little systematic guidance for the parents to make the best of the very early and the preschool years. It is my sincere hope that the guidance given in this book so far will have provided a firm foundation on which you can now build these new and essential skills.

First we do well to remember that just as there is a range of intellectual ability between dull and bright in any group of normal children, so there will always be in a group of children with similar handicaps, complicated in the case of the deaf/blind by the additional factor of differing degrees of sight or hearing loss. So although I hope it may be possible to begin using the programmes suggested in this Chapter well before your child enters school—before 5—the actual age is less important than knowing what to do when the time comes and the child is ready.

78

What each child achieves will vary also. For some deaf/blind children the programmes will lead to reading, writing and number and, perhaps, ultimately to as independant an adult life as a deaf/blind person can expect. For others the skills they learn through the programmes may represent the sum total of their learning during schooldays, yet is enough to give them an ability to enjoy their environment, to occupy themselves and perhaps to succeed later in a simple work situation. For a few only some of the items will become meaningful and as a result they will enjoy life at a simple level the better for having experience of the materials and the loving patience and attention of the person who used them with them.

The programmes have been arranged under three headings:
Pre-reading activities
Pre-writing activities
Pre-number activities

They are organised on the basis of the present-day approach to the education of handicapped children, relative to the basic perceptual, motor and cognitive skills, which, together with language, most children possess by the time they start school and without which learning, in its academic sense, cannot occur. These skills are made up of a number of specific skills which emerge slowly in sequence (just as we have seen in all other areas) and become integrated with each other to enable the child to deal with more complex learning situations. Since the deaf/blind child has such limited channels through which to receive information, providing him with materials carefully structured to give him experience of the specific skills and then the integrated skills, ensures that we do not waste time or miss out essential steps in the sequence.
Basic perceptual skills are those by which information received through hearing, sight, touch, smell and taste is recognised by sound, colour/shape/picture/size, texture/size, odour, taste. Basic cognitive skills are those which enable us to organise, remember and use the information we receive (a) by comparison of similarities and differences, (b) by grouping in terms of alike or not alike, of sequences, direction and in association and (c) by relationships i.e. number/quantity. Basic motor skills with which we are concerned here are those requiring fine motor co-ordination to allow the hand and eye to work together through a sequence of tasks such as threading, cutting, using crayons etc., ultimately leading to the ability to write. Put more simply—if you cannot learn the difference between a circle and a square you will not be able to distinguish between the letters a and b etc., if you cannot learn the difference between the sounds made by a bell and a drum, you will certainly not learn the difference between the speech sounds

say 'cat' and 'cap' and therefore would not be able to associate these correctly when reading or writing these words. If you are not aware of the ordering of things—sequencing—you will not be able to recognise the difference in meaning between 'cat' and 'act'; equally so if you cannot draw a straight line and a circle, you certainly will not be able to use these in the various ways in which they are combined to enable us to represent sounds by writing. Perhaps these few examples will enable you to realise the importance of these specific skills for all children, but particularly for those with limited opportunity for receiving the information in the first place.

Each of the three programmes contains a number of items, to be worked through preferably in the order in which they are set out. Each item contains a series of activities which are set out in order of difficulty and consequently MUST be worked through in that order. Ideally one activity from each programme would make a suitable daily session, but you would need to work up to this gradually and of course you could have two such sessions if your child really enjoys it.

The activities are divided into those used informally and the formal kind that require you to sit down beside your child and work with him. The child needs to have had some experience and show some understanding of the informal activities before beginning the formal activities. If your child has a home teacher or attends a preschool programme, the teacher can use the formal activities parallel with the parent using the informal ones—but the formal activities can and should be used by parents when no teacher is available or inconjunction with the teacher. These activities complement each other—as must teacher and parent. The parent/child and teacher/pupil relationship is a most important factor in this work—it is to be hoped that parents do not have to fulfil both roles but will, from the beginning of this stage of intensive play and learning, share the task with a thoughtful and knowledgeable teacher. Upon these relationships depends success or failure. The adult has to create, structure and use these experiences for development and learning, but often it is the child who provides the clues to the direction to be taken and parent and teacher alike must be ready to snatch at the right moment to introduce or consolidate a new experience. Consistency of approach is essential—mother and teacher must have the same goals and each know how the other plans to get there. They must both see that help is given when the child needs it, never after a task has been mastered and share the attitude "we will help him until he can do it himself".

The informal activities need just as careful planning as the formal ones —it is no good giving a deaf/blind child a bag of mixed buttons to sort until he has learned by sorting them one at a time the differences in colour, shape, size or texture etc. It is no good showing him how to put one spoon at each place at the table on Mondays and Fridays only

—he must do it every day until you know he can do it by himself. Whatever you play in the way of formal activities keep it short and use the same material until the concept or skill is learned, then use other similar materials in the same way to give him opportunity for practice and to show that his learning is not tied to the material itself but can be used in all circumstances requiring the particular skill.

Always make sure you have all the things you need for a session immediately to hand. Nothing destroys concentration (yours and the childs) more quickly than having to leave him to get something you have forgotten. Often the same material can be used for all the activities you plan to do in a session. A normal child when he plays with, say, bricks does lots of things with them—makes a train, puts the colours together, fits them into other things, throws them, hides them and so on and in the process has used a number of skills. The items in the programmes lend themselves to this kind of organisation and some Sample Plans showing how to build your daily session of formal activities round a particular type of material are included.

Teaching techniques. One thing that gives most encouragement to learning is its reward—for the normal child his pleasure in doing and succeeding is often enough to make him want to learn more. This is not usually so for the deaf/blind child, we must provide the reward for effort and success in a form that is meaningful to him—a hug, a sweet, play with a favourite toy kept specially for the purpose, a game he likes, something he gets *immediately* he has finished his task. In time when an activity becomes familiar and he enjoys it, rewarding in this deliberate fashion can be dropped out gradually and only given when a new or more difficult task is introduced.

Some children have great difficulty in paying attention to the task in hand and really the only way to help them is to be firm, make the task very brief to begin with and insist that it is completed before he is allowed to move away. You might just put out a red car and a blue car together with a red box and a blue box—and help him to put the cars into the matching box. If you do this regularly for several days you will almost certainly find that he accepts he must do this in order to get down from the table and that is the time to insist that he sort two cars of each colour. It is generally the familiarity of the task and its regularity that sets these children with poor attention span going, and it is usually not long before they are able to concentrate for periods that, whilst still short, are long enough to provide a useful learning experience.

To begin with formal activities should be done with the child on the parent/teacher's lap so that there is a measure of control and ease in manipulating the child's hands to do the task correctly. Later on you can sit beside the child or opposite him if he is able to lipread. If your child has a hearing aid and/or glasses it is to be hoped that he wears them all day, but he must certainly have them on for any periods which can be regarded directed play.

It has been observed that some of the rubella deaf/blind children who are very very distracted by any light sources in the room and attend to this in preference to the materials you offer them, work better in a darkened room where the light source can be controlled i.e. a spot light can be so arranged that it throws a circle of light on to the table and the object to be played with is placed in this circle. Toys which themselves light up when played with—a shape posting box which you can rig with a battery and light bulb at the bottom which lights up when the shapes drop down, the Litebright toy or similarly made commercial items. For others an apparatus to be placed on the table to act as a "tunnel" which would restrict the child's visual field to the table and the teacher opposite him. No two deaf/blind children are alike, some may need special help of this kind to begin with to help them to concentrate others may quickly, and gladly, give up their obsession for light. Start by offering the play material at a table which is in a good light but has no very strong direct rays to the front of the child. If difficulties arise, watch the position of light when the child plays by himself and using this as your guide experiment with controlled lighting until you find that in which he responds best. Any devices which encourage the child to play are well worth the making and can generally be made at home to suit your particular circumstances.

Points to remember

1. Play session NOT lesson. Short and regular.
2. These sessions do not take the place of other kinds of play—the child must continue to have lots of experience of movement, sand, water and clay, large building and constructional toys.
3. Always communicate with your child during these sessions. Give instructions:
   spoken in language understood by the child, or
   signed in language understood by the child, or
   finger spelled understood by the child, or
   gestured using pointing, nodding etc, or
   by showing him how and then letting him copy, or
   manipulating his hands
   If the child is not able to respond to one or other of these means of instructing him, he is not ready to begin formal sessions.
4 For the child with vision for colour this provides his main clue together with shape—for the child who has poor vision texture must replace colour.
5. Know exactly what you are going to do during a session, but if the child's response suggests an opportunity to teach something out-

side the plan but which is useful, be prepared to use the material with flexibility.

6. When you have gathered together the materials for a session place these in a box or on a tray and put them in a place to which you can take the child to get them with you to carry to the table where you will play with them. When finished let him help you take them back to this place. Fetching them helps him to antici-pate the activity—it also creates a situation in which, by pointing to or taking you to the place he can tell you he would like to play with the materials set aside for the special sessions. Our ultimate aim must be to bring him to the stage when he can use these ma-terials on his own, but we must be with him until we are certain such play is meaningful.

7. Materials used for play sessions must not be given to the child for free play.

8. To 'reach' a deaf/blind child you must get down to his level —bend your knees, sit on the floor beside him, on a small chair beside him—you must come to the level of his face, for he cannot reach up to yours.

9. If you are a parents taking on the formal (and the informal) play sessions, be confident. Parents are all teachers by nature —otherwise how would children know so much by the time they are ready for school?

10. There are other methods that could be used but no one method is necessarily the right one—you must have some overall plan, but if you are successful it is as likely to be due to increasing develop-ment and maturation of the child, your patience and determi-nation, the child's effort than to the method itself.

PRE-READING PROGRAMMES

In order to understand the importance of the specific skills set out in these programmes, we need to appreciate where in the develop-mental sequence reading comes. Reading is a form of communication which follows listening/speaking and precedes writing. In the Chapter on Communication we considered language in its two auditory forms —receptive (listening) and expressive (speaking), what we are now concerned with is language in one of its two similar visual forms —receptive or reading. The other visual form is, of course, expressive or writing. Just as listening must occur for speaking to be possible, so must a child learn to read before learning to write, the latter also involving the fine motor skills set out in the pre-writing programme.

Children do not jump from the auditory to the visual system, the visual has to be linked with the auditory and a long period of speaking what he is reading precedes the ability to read silently. So it is important in a *pre*-reading programme to stress the auditory components of language which have a counterpart in its visual form. The deaf/blind child with useful sight will, we hope, eventually learn to read large print and when he is learning to do this will refer back to speech or his sign system. The deaf/blind child who has no useful sight and needs a tactile method of communication also needs a tactile method of reading, that is, braille. He must learn to match the pattern of the braille dots with the sign he has learned to interpret when it is given on his hand. The components common to the auditory and visual forms of language are also common to the tactile form and these are:

(a) Single units—separate sounds, letters and dot patterns.
(b) Groups of single units—groups of sounds which form words, letters which form words and dot patterns which form words.
(c) A series of (b) in a sequence—the spoken sentence, written or braille sentence.

So the specific skills we need to encourage are the discrimination and memory for:

(a) Single units in terms of differences i.e. the red cars go in the red box, the blue cars in the blue box. This is visual, the same exercises must also be done with tactual and auditory material.
in terms of similarities i.e. out of a group of different objects find one that is like the one in my hand.
(b) Groups of units—all the things that are red or not red, all the things that make a sound or do not, things that go together (association)—brush and comb.
(c) Things in sequence—concerned with the order of things i.e. copying a pattern of colours, textures or rhythmic sounds. This also involves direction for sequencing is always done from left to right in preparation for the direction in which we read.

We need to use a variety of materials so that from these experiences our deaf/blind children will acquire "concepts"—the name given to describe the general headings under which we recognise, organise and remember the things in our world i.e. once the child has a "concept" of cup he will be able to recognise it whether it is large, small, china, plastic, plain, patterned etc., etc.

In suggesting these programmes I must stress that they represent the kind of activities all children do in the preschool years, there is no set rule that they must ALL be done. They provide examples from which you can develop many more activities providing additional opportunities for practicing the skills they teach. What is most important is that you and your child share some activities each day and that these activities are of the kind that help him learn useful concepts. How much he learns, whilst affected by the degree and severity of his handicap, will also depend on his own personal characteristics—his interests, temperament, abilities, energy level, his family and their way of life. Your own acceptance of him, the time you give to this kind of specific help and your recognition of the importance of these activities, will influence his learning.

The programmes are arranged under the separate headings of Visual, and/or Tactile, and Auditory activities in order to draw the child's attention to one aspect at a time. Of course more than one sensory channel is always being used and as you progress through the separate programmes you will become aware of the overlapping and in time learn to give emphasis to the integration as well as the separate use.

VISUAL AND TACTILE ACTIVITIES

1. Colour and Texture

Use colour and texture programmes for the partially sighted, texture only for the child with no useful sight.

Informal Activities

A. SORTING

If you have lots of evidence that your child is aware of colour or texture differences, i.e. shows an obvious preference for all red toys or all objects with rough surfaces, you can begin on the programmes below. If you are uncertain, playing the following little game may prove he is aware of these aspects or may help him make the discrimination.

Colour Sit with your child at a table and have two upturned beakers, one red and one blue. Let him *see* you hide a sweet or small favourite toy (anything you know he will want to get hold of) under the red beaker. Show him how to find it and let him have it. Then hide another sweet (or same object) again, always under the red beaker and encourage him to get it for himself. The sweet must always go under the same colour, but you can alter the position of the beakers if you wish.

When he goes without hesitation to the red one no matter where it is placed, you will know he recognises colour. It may take quite a time for your child to learn this, but do it for a few minutes every day and don't give up.

Texture Use the same technique as for colour, but cover one of the two beakers with a rough material (sandpaper) leaving the other plain, and letting him feel you put the sweet or toy underneath.

Materials Bricks, cotton reels (painted), buttons, balls of wool, toy cars, etc., of various colours.

Suitable items from the above which can be covered with such materials as velvet, fur, leather, plastic, or made of differing materials, i.e. foam rubber, polystyrene, wood and so on.

Cardboard or plastic trays of the kind you have when you buy packed foods, lined with coloured paper or texture which the child is to match.

85

Procedure   To begin with offer the child a choice of two things only, and make sure there is a big contrast between them i.e. sorts blue and red, not red and orange, or sorts fur and sandpaper, not fur and velvet. As your child understands the task, and when he has sorted a large number of sets of two things, you can try him on sorting three items and then four and there can be less difference between.

(i)   Sit child on your lap and have two trays matched with the colour or texture you want him to sort on the table in front of you. Give him a brick of each of the two colours or textures and show him how they go into the matching tray. Hand him more bricks, one at a time and show him how to look for the colour of feel the texture and then place in the correct tray.

(ii)   Using an old shoebox make two divisions by using two pieces of different coloured paper or textured material stuck on the top and in each of which you make a slit. Make two sets of small cards to fit slit and cover these with matching coloured paper or textured material—the child has to select from the cards and post through matching slit. When he can manage two divisions, make another box with three divisions and proceed as above.

(iii)   All the materials under the Pre-writing activities used for threading are also useful for colour matching and when he is proficient in both separately, you can combine the two skills by getting him to thread rings, beads etc of a particular colour. The rings or beads can be texture covered for the child with no useful vision.

Formal Activities
B. PATTERN COPYING

Materials   Small bricks of different colours or covered with different textures, 2 of each. 3" square cards coloured or covered with different textures, 2 of each. Pegboards, large then small pegs.

Procedure   Begin with choice of two only, increase gradually.

(i)   Adult has one set, child has the other, adult places one on table and shows child how to place his matching brick/card on top. When child can do this adult places two different bricks etc. on table and child matches both—and so on up to four.

(ii)   Prepare a sheet of paper (or card) by sticking on it squares (two, then three and up to 5) of different coloured paper or texture. The child has to place his matching one over the one stuck on the paper. These should be in a row to begin with and then in pattern.

(iii)   Adult makes a brick patterns of two (working up to 6) Patterns can be horizontal or built up, can represent squares, oblongs, steps, letter shapes etc., etc.

(iv)   As for (iii) but use pegs and pegboard.

C. SAME AND DIFFERENT

Materials Any of the materials used for sorting and patterns with which the child is reasonably familiar.

Procedure

(i) From a number of mixed items child has to find one or all that are similar to the one you have in your hand.

(ii) Out of six items of which 5 are the same and one different, he has to pick out the one that is different.

D. SEQUENCING

Materials Bricks or cards of differing colour or texture. Small cars all of one kind but different colours or of varying kinds, (also aeroplanes or boats, little dolls or any small material that interests the child. Outdoor material like acorns, leaves conkers can also be used at a later stage) You need two sets of each.

Procedure

(i) To get him used to the idea of sequencing begin with some sheets of paper or card upon which you have two squares drawn with a brightly coloured felt pen or outlined with fine string. (work up to 5 in a row gradually). You and the child each have a card—you place a brick, card or object in the left hand square he places a similar one in his lefthand square. You place a similar one or a different one in the right hand square, he does the same. When he understands this routine, you fill both squares at once, left then right and he follows suit.

(ii) Once he gets the idea of matching his sequence to yours in the left to right direction, you can dispense with the guide squares and just set out the line of items for him to immitate.

E. MEMORY

Materials Any of the materials used above. The bottom half of an old shoebox.

Procedure

(i) Give child 2 objects. Show him or let him feel one that is similar to one of his two, then put it underneath the upturned shoebox and "ask" him to give you his one that is the same as the one under the box.

Progress by giving him 3 then 4 objects from which to chose. Then put two under the box and ask him to give you both from his group. Then ask for 3.

(ii) Two sets of three different objects. Put your set out on table and hide from child's view with cardboard shield. Take one of your objects and hold it in your hand so that the child cannot see which one it is, remove the cardboard shield and ask child to look at or feel his set, then look at or feel your remaining two—and from this tell you, point to or give you from his group the one which matches that in your hand. This is Kims Game and when the child can play it with understanding, you can remove his set of objects and he must guess which is in your hand and "tell" you by naming, gesturing its use, or giving you the appropriate sign.

(iii) At an advanced stage Memory and Sequencing can be brought together by showing a sequence of objects or coloured cards (or textures) for a brief period, then removing from his view and asking him to reproduce the sequence from memory.

2. Shape

The partially sighted child needs to be made aware of shape both visually and tactually, the child with no useful sight must have corners, curves and straight edges very carefully stressed for him by touch.

Informal Activities

The following activities help children to become aware of shape:

(i) rolling balls, hoops, tins, jar tops etc., along the floor, down slopes etc.

(ii) wind and unwind wool, on reels or square section spindles.

(iii) simple inset board with one circle and one square—later on one with triangle as well.

(iv) playing "ring a ring of roses", "round and round the garden" etc.

(v) draw attention to things in the environment that are round and square—lots of kitchen utensils are round and square, we eat round and square biscuits, stools can be both round and square and so on.

Formal Activities

F. SORTING

Materials   Circles, squares, triangles and oblongs in plastic, wood, or card.

Procedure

(i) Circles and squares into round and square boxes.

(ii) Various shapes to be sorted into piles of same shape.

(iii) Placing correct shapes onto card on which matching shapes have been drawn and coloured black.

(iv) Same as (iii) but shapes on paper are only outlined.

(v) Add cards of diamond and cross and use in same way as (i) to (iv)

88

(vi) Circles and squares cut out in cardboard and with a hole in the centre for stitching the radii.

(vii) Child makes patterns with coloured sticky backed paper shapes (which can be bought ready cut, but made more cheaply if you buy coloured sheets and cut out your own shapes).

(viii) When child shows a good awareness of shape you can introduce formboards with 6 shapes, working up to those with 12. There are also available plastic inset boards with animal shapes, common object shapes and double shapes. Simple jigsaws done back to front (no picture) encourage a child to notice shape, particularly as he must match the shape of the piece he holds, not with the jigsaw shape, but with the hole into which it fits.

G. SEQUENCING AND MEMORY

Procedure is as for colours and texture—using black shapes stuck on cards in ones, twos and threes i.e. one circle; circle, square or circle triangle; circle, square, triangle; circle, circle, square; and any number of combinations.

(i) Child places in order on card, left to right.

(ii) Child sees briefly and then places in sequence on table from memory.

When child becomes proficient in colour, texture and shape discrimination, you can combine all three elements and match, sequence and remember for colour and shape, texture and colour shape and texture.

3. Pictures (For the child with partial sight)

Matching Before a child learns to match pictures you must be certain he can match objects. Both number and visual/tactile programmes have included some object matching, but if you are in any doubt as to his ability to do this, let him do some simple sorting with the objects you intend to use for the first pictures—i.e. familiar things like ball, spoon, toothbrush, etc., using the 2 tray method and sorting say up to 4 each of 2 kinds of objects.

Then match similar objects but made of different materials, i.e. wood, plastic, metal spoons.

(i) Using the same objects as for matching, trace round the outline of the objects with finger and then draw round the object *with the child*. This should be done a number of times immediately after the matching activity. When it has been done a fair number of times the child is encouraged to pick up the correct object and put it on the drawing. After establishing this for a number of objects, a set of drawings should be kept and the child should be able to match objects to the drawings without having to draw round it first.

(ii) Match outline of single object cut out and mounted on plywood with the real object.

(iii) Match mounted cut-out to picture.

(iv) Trace round outlines of picture with finger (these outlines can be made more obvious by lining with thick felt pen or with wool, alternatively the picture can be mounted, cut out and then mounted again on to a background so that it is raised).

(v) Working model "pictures" may be used, i.e. "flat" people with arms and legs jointed with paper clips; wheels on pictures of cars made to turn, bonnets to lift etc.

(vi) Cardboard shapes can be used to slide into gloves, socks etc.

(vii) When child has had considerable experience of the above activities you can begin to use real pictures cut out from picture books such as the Ladybird ones making sure that they are of things relevant to your child's own experience for which you can give him the real objects, i.e. cup, orange, hairbrush, comb etc. This is about the time you can begin to introduce a few miniature things by gradually reducing the size of the objects you use—you can first match an ordinary cup to the picture, then a small coffee cup and down to the small dolls teaset type. You can do this with saucers, plates, dishes, spoons, socks, shoes, gloves, balls and so on. Once a child appreciates miniatures as representative of the real object, you have a much wider variety of objects to picture matching materials in dolls house furniture, cooking and kitchen utensils, dolls clothes and other toy models of everyday things. The pictures should be cut out and mounted on card and covered with clear contact or fablon to help to keep them clean and less likely to tear.

Progression

(a) Objects that match exactly.
     Objects that match less exactly.
     Variation in colour, pattern etc. for more advanced sets.

(b) Clear or plain background.
     Less clear background.
     Complicated foreground.

Best size is about 4″ × 4″—any larger may be difficult to see. Each set should have about 12 pairs to allow for 3, 4 and 5 pairs for practice or two sets of 6 for more advanced.

(viii) When the child can match picture to object and object to picture adequately, introduce the idea of matching an object with 2 pictures—set out on the table in the following way:

Object
Picture
Picture

making sure you draw attention to the fact that not only do the pictures both match the object, but also match each other. This leads naturally to matching pairs of pictures.

Sequencing   Same procedure as for colour and texture.

Memory

(i) *Objects* One set of objects on a table close by and another set on your lap. Show or let child feel object and ask him to get you the matching one from the table. He will need showing how to do this at first. Gradually put the table further away from you so child has further to go and longer to remember what it is he has to get. Ultimately the table should be in another room to which child goes by himself to fetch the object.

(ii) Let child see you place 2 familiar pictures under a piece of cardboard. Show him a copy of one of these pictures for about as long as it takes you to count to ten, then turn away from his view and ask him to lift the cover and find one like the one you showed him. Repeat with the second picture. Gradually increase the number of pictures used to 5.

Other uses for pictures

Once the child understands the meaning of pictures you can use them for the following activities:

(i) Show him pictures of things you use and ask him to gesture their use i.e. hairbrush—child pretends to brush his hair, spoon—child puts hand to mouth.

(ii) Show him pictures of people in action and ask him to immitate i.e. child sees picture of person sitting down—he sits down, of someone jumping—he jumps, and so on. (Pictures of stick-men are quite useful for demonstrating actions)

Conclusion   From an awareness of shapes the partially sighted deaf child will progress to the discrimination of letters and when he is able to group these in a sequence, i.e. c a t, he is shown how to match this with the picture of a cat and to associate it with its auditory or signed equivalent. This is where reading readiness is completed and real reading begins. A deaf/blind child reaching this stage will without doubt be in a school and it is for his teacher to guide you on how to complement her methods of teaching him to read.

For the child with such poor sight that he cannot see pictures, we work through his awareness of shapes to recognition of patterns through touch—pegboard pattern copying i.e. squares, triangles, letter shapes first from a model, then from memory and several patterns in sequence from memory—leading up to braille. The actual teaching of braille is for the expert whose help you must seek when your child shows these skills—again he should be in school well before he reaches this stage. Your task is to get your child started on the early exercises that lay the foundations for this later work—getting him started requires a lot of patience. You may find that having made good progress, he will then remain stationery before making another spurt. However if you keep him interested he is bound to progress and this is more important that the rate at which he goes.

Pictures provide opportunity for training another important aspect of reading—termed "closure" that is being able to recognise things when they not whole and be able to match them up when separated into parts. i.e.

> Pictures cut into two, give child one part, he has to select the one that fits, or,
> Cards on which either the left or right half is blank, child choses the card to fit the blank half.

There are some excellent commercially produced cards of pictures of everyday objects—a teapot without a handle, child finds card with handle on it and fits them together. You can make these yourself if you are good at drawing.

Using this technique with pictures of people helps children to learn body image and you should present them in the following order:

> 2 pieces horizontally
> 3 pieces horizontally
> 2 pieces vertically
> 3 pieces vertically
> 2 pieces diagonally
> 4 and 5 pieces cut various ways.

For the child with very poor sight use pictures raised by outlining with string or wool, or raised in silhouette by sticking on various textures to match together.

Language

The important words to stress during these pre-reading exercises are these connected with colour, texture and shape. Objects should be named and when the object is matched to picture, the name transferred. The phrases "give me" and "find" should be used where appropriate and when the direction of the movement can be emphasised, such prepositions as on, in and under.

Additional tips

One way of anchoring material for the child with poor sight who tends to knock things off the table easily is to stick small pieces of magnetic tape on the bottom of the material and work on a thin sheet of metal to which the material will then hold. Alternatively a felt-covered board or tray for playing on helps to prevent material slipping.

Occasionally a child has difficulty in seeing because the gap in the cataract is not central and this can be overcome by lifting the material at an angle on a stand or sometimes by using it on the floor.

The importance of continually reinforcing tactile training cannot be overstressed. Tactile clues are important to all children with the dual handicap, but whereas those with very poor sight are forced to depend on tactual experiences, those with some sight often do not pay attention to the feel of things unless deliberately encouraged to do so. In addition to the tactile experiences provided within the prereading programmes, the following are also useful:

Playing in water that is hot or cold, ordinary or soapy.

Playing with things that are wet and dry, damp, cold, warm etc.

Handling food that is smooth, sticky, crumbly, thin, thick, hot, cold, icy.

Handling paper—thin, thick, tissue, rolled, corregated etc.

Awareness of water in cup, bath, sink, out of tap, teapot, watering can rose, sieve etc.

Playing tug of war with rope, towel, winding wool, string, raffia, cotton, wire etc.

Feeling things in the garden—chestnuts in husk, leaves of trees, grass blades, flowers, barks of trees, pebbles, etc.

Feeling knobs, switches, vibration from hoover, washing machine, spinner, radio.

Feeling living things—cats, dogs, rabbits, tortoise, caterpillar etc.

Feeling objects which are hidden behind a screen or in a bag or box with holes in for hands to be put through to feel—child either has to name the one he feels or to find from matching set, or this can be done with a set of the same objects but different in size.

AUDITORY TRAINING ACTIVITIES

Whether a deaf/blind child will eventually use his residual hearing to listen to, interpret and reproduce speech sounds or only for the enjoyment of gross sounds and/or their vibration, we should spend some time each day giving him specific auditory experiences over and above those which he receives as you talk to him in the course of everyday routines. Very few children are totally deaf—if they do not have sufficient hearing to be able to discriminate the fine differences in speech sounds they are still likely to hear and enjoy sounds made by such things as bells, cymbals, clackers, drums, horn, whistle, squeeze toys, crickets and various percussion instruments. Some children, unless stimulated, may just not make use of the hearing they possess. An audiogram shows how much hearing a child has, but does not show you how much he hears, so we must provide opportunity to hear all sorts of things and find out what he enjoys and see that where this can add to his knowledge of the world, it is used for this purpose.

If you have been successful in stimulating interest in sound in the ways suggested in previous chapters, your deaf/blind child should by now be showing an awareness and enjoyment of sound by turning to its source (a door banging) putting his hand on the source (on your face when you are speaking, on the radio etc. for vibration) imitating it (copying a sound you make, repeating his own sounds) or by operating some noisemaking toy repeatedly (banging a drum). If he is going to be able to learn to speak eventually these auditory training activities will help him. If he will have to communicate by another means, they will enable him to appreciate other sounds in his environment. In particular the sequencing and rhythm activities will help to reinforce the skills which are important to reading.

Informal
1. Play with toys that have a sound element, teddies that growl, talking dolls, humming tops, squeaky toys. Fisher Action music boxes are ideal in that they are dual purpose—as well as listening, the child has to turn a handle to operate them. Home made shakers made from transparent plastic bottles or cartons filled with rice, beans, buttons etc. make nice noises. Kitchenware—aluminium pieplate and spoon, saucepan lids to bang together and so on (if you can bear it!) Crunchy paper.
2. *Discrimination*. (sound and no sound)
   Child has to put a brick (or any other suitable material) into a box each time he hears a bang on a drum (or any other sound which you know he hears)
   It often takes a long time for the child to learn to play this game—it is really teaching him to listen—but he must learn it before you can go onto any of the other activities.
   Method   First let the child see what happens by demonstrating. Then taking his hand in yours pick up a brick, draw his attention to the drum being banged and as you bang it, put the brick in the box. The sound and the action must occur together. When you feel he is ready let him gradually take over the action himself. Finally the drum is banged out of his sight and he is expected to put the brick in the box in response to hearing only.
   Once he understands the game, you can use a variety of materials and lots of different sounds to keep his interest and increase his attention to a wider range of sounds.
3. *Environmental sounds*
   Draw his attention to such sounds as knocking at the door, ringing the doorbell, the telephone bell, hoover (he may enjoy helping you because of the vibration or maybe follow the sound as you move around the room with it) water running from a tap, when the toilet is flushed—as many of these things that can be made meaningful

to him through their sound element as possible.

Dancing with him in your arms when you have a record or radio on.

If he will move towards a source of music, put a transistor radio in different positions near him and see if he will locate it—move it further away gradually.

Stamp on the floor with your feet as you approach him—this is a valuable clue to the child with very poor sight as it alerts him to the fact that someone is near him.

Shake a box (or tin etc) with no toy in it, put a toy in it with the child's hand on your own, shake box to make sound, open box and discover.

Noisemaking toys are good for encouraging gestures—waving hand from side to side to indicate a bell, using the hand like a hammer for the drum, or shaking the hand for a rattle.

Formal

4. *Associating sound with its source* (What made the sound, which thing made which sound)

   Use noisemakers with a big contrast to begin with i.e. a drum and a squeaker, letting them become more similar so that the discrimination is more difficult, i.e. three bells of differing pitch).

   Method

   (a) Use 2 bells 2 rattles—put one of each in front of child, you have the other two and sound them one at a time behind his back—he has to select the one he hears and you keep sounding it until he does.

   (b) Use 3 noisemakers—have on a table behind child, you sound one, he has to turn and select the one he heard.

   (c) You and the child each have a noisemaker, child imitates the sounds you make—you may sound it once, or twice, for a long time or only briefly.

   (d) You and the child each have an instrument (a drum or chime bar is best) you bang a rhythm—very simple rhythms i.e.

   dah dah (long sounds)
   di di (short sounds)
   dah didi
   didi dah
   dah didah

   The child should feel these rythms by placing his fingertips on the drum when you beat it out. You can also take his hand and play them out on different parts of his body.

   At an advanced level the child is encouraged to continue repeating a rhythm, and to do all the above activities in terms of loud/soft and high/low—but probably only the child with hearing for speech.

95

All the above activities will take any deaf/blind child a long time to learn and a lot of patient demonstration and taking him through the actions many many times will precede his ability to do them on his own. They are important to him, they will give him pleasure and help to develop an awareness to sound that will be valuable to him as additional clues in a variety of ways all through his life.

For the child who is responding to sound as a partially hearing child all the activities recommended for preschool deaf children will be valid and you will be helped to use these by the peripetetic teacher of the deaf who should be a frequent visitor to your house during the preschool years.

PRE-WRITING PROGRAMMES

When we delightedly watch a child first write his own name we rarely think of the hundred and one activities using his hands and eyes in co-ordination that have prepared him for this moment. He has learned a great many skills in the process and these are useful to him in lots of ways in addition to writing. So far as deaf/blind children are concerned whilst we must accept that only a few of them will acquire writing skills and use these to record their thoughts, the same handeye co-ordination is necessary for the many other activities and occupations which are within the capabilities of the deaf/blind children who do not learn to write. So writing itself is a long term aim and our immediate aim is to encourage the acquisition of the sub-skills.

It is impossible and indeed it would be wrong to try to design handeye co-ordination programmes which do involve the perceptual skills, for integration is very important. What you must remember is that, for instance you can ask a child to thread beads as a handeye co-ordination task, you cannot ask him to thread beads by colour until you have worked through the colour matching exercises under the pre-reading programmes. The more of these programmes you do, the more you will see how they all overlap and you will become proficient at getting several aspects of learning out of very simple material.

When your child is using crayons or pencils, make sure he is sitting square to the table and is comfortable. Use the non-dominent hand to steady the paper he is working on—also if the paper slips about, anchor it down with some cellotape at the corners. If a child is using an easel or wall blackboard see that it is at the right height and that he does not have to reach up to it. Do not deny them paints because they are messy—spread an old waterproof ground-sheet on the floor and use one of Daddy's old shirts to protect the child's own clothes.

Language   As these programmes are basically motor they provide fine opportunities for teaching such concepts as:

up, down, across, round, along, go, stop etc.

Informal activities
Bricks
The very first game children enjoy which encourages handeye co-ordination is building bricks into towers and knocking them down. Show the child, take him through the movements then let him knock down your tower and eventually build the tower himself and knock it down. When he has reached this stage it is added fun to see how many bricks can be built up before it falls down, to take turns at building and knocking down each other's tower, and seeing if you can also blow it down.

Threading   Some experience of threading has already been gained with apparatus like rings on sticks recommended in phases 2 and 3.

These can be continued, reducing the size of the stick and the hole in the stick, and variety can be added by varying the angle of the stick by holding it sideways, longwise, near or far from the child, to one side or the other or so that he can thread from the bottom or the top.

Progress to large bead threading (square then round) first on plastic covered wire, then on cord (or shoelace) with the tags lengthened with cellotape binding. Beads covered with various textures should be provided for the child with very poor sight When he can thread by himself, bring in the perceptual skills by:

(i)   Threading by colour (or texture).

(ii)   Threading by alternate colours (one red, one blue, one red or one rough, one smooth and so on).

(iii)   Threading to a pattern either to match one you have done or to a pattern illustrated on a card.

Formboards, jigsaws. Formboards have been mentioned under **SHAPE** and of course they encourage handeye co-ordination. Large jigsaws with lift-out pieces are useful and for the child with poor sight, the lift out pieces can be covered with different textures. Posting boxes of which a variety are produced commercially combine awareness of shape with fine motor skills. For the child with an intense interest in light, fixing a light in the bottom of the posting box that is operated by the shape falling through the hole to the bottom provides incentive and reward.

Water and Sand   Pouring from one container into another. The container receiving the sand or water needs to be wider to start with and as the child manages better, it can be smaller so that he needs greater skill in directing the material. When he can pour reasonably well give him every opportunity of pouring out his own milk or juice.

When child reaches the stage of copying or tracing shapes and letters, sand spread lightly over a large tray presents a medium for practicing these skills with the finger or stick.

Ball play Sitting on floor opposite each other, feet touching, roll ball back and forth from child to adult within the boundary formed by the legs.

Rolling a ball between two obstacles.
Rolling a ball to knock down skittles.
Throwing a ball into a box.
Throwing a ball through a hoop.
Throwing a ball under a rope.
Throwing a ball to another person.
Catching a ball.

(Use balls of various sizes)

Crayoning/chalking Random crayoning or chalking on paper or blackboard with horizontal and vertical strokes, leading on to circular movements. Take child through the movements until you feel he is making some effort himself, then lessen your guidance. Once this activity is learned, it is usually enjoyed and even a blind child likes to cover a blackboard with chalk. For the partially sighted child with good colour awareness crayoning on different coloured paper i.e. white on black, red on blue etc., adds interest and the near-blind child can crayon on paper of different textures i.e. embossed wallpaper, fine sandpaper etc. Sugar paper is the ideal material, but newspaper is better than nothing. Cellotape to table or fix in a frame to prevent tearing.

Filling in shape templates (cut out in 6″ squares of plastic or thin wood —circle, square and triangle) with crayon or chalk gives the child his first experience in keeping within bounds. Take his finger round the inside of the shape first, then clip the template to the paper with a couple of bulldog clips and show the child how to run the crayon round the outside before he does the filling in. For interest the crayoned shapes can be cut out and pasted onto a backsheet either in pattern or to make a picture of say a train (4 circles for the wheels and squares for the engine and carriages) or a house (a square and a triangle)—there are endless possibilities, both for shape awareness and for language.

The pieces cut from the plastic or wood sheet to make the templates can be kept and used, later on, for drawing round.

Plasticine Rolled out into long thin sausage:
Shape into circle.
Pull in half and make a cross, into 4 and make a square, into 3 and make a triangle.

Again when the stage of copying and tracing letters is reached, you can use plasticine sticks and circles to draw attention to the differences between p, d, q and b, and to practice the other letter shapes.

Dough This is one of the ideal materials for fine motor skills. It can be made of the bits left over from your own cooking, or made up of three parts flour, one part salt and water and a little oil (the latter not to be eaten) If at first the child does not like the feel of the dough, warm it in your hands and keep it well floured. Let him feel it, pat it, poke it, flatten it, roll it (with hands or small rolling pin) until he is quite familiar with it. When he enjoys handling it—and he will if you give him time,—he can have sets of cutters to cut out various sized circles and place these each in a little patty pan which you have laid in rows on a baking sheet. To add interest when the dough rounds are in the patty pans, he can place a currant, cherry or something similar in the centre of each.

Using non-toxic food colouring you can make the dough different colours and it is fun to cut little pink rounds and put these on big green rounds and so on. If you use real dough (not the salt based kind) it can be cooked and eaten—letting him see it go into the oven and when it comes out feeling the difference in texture, in smell and enjoy something he has helped to make.

Pasting Tap-water Paste is a good medium—give the child a chance to feel this and to use his fingers to spread it on if he likes, or a brush. Sticking newspaper onto newspaper is a good start, and later he can stick on to a firm base pieces of coloured or textured paper, or material. Using the firmer paste that can be purchased and squeezed out onto the paper, the child can be encouraged to follow a trail by sticking onto it such things as dried beans, shells, woodshavings etc., and later to making his own patterns.

Tearing newspaper, putting it into water and squeezing it, sprinkling it with polycell, then using to mould into balls, shapes etc., (paper mache).

Bubbles Using washingup liquid, blow bubbles and get child to pop by poking with his finger.

Small beads or similar Picking these up and dropping them into a bottle.

Other ideas for hand skills Bolts fixed on to a board, child fits on nuts.

Boxes set in plaster of paris in shallow tray—child fits on lids.

Undoing parcels—wrapped in paper, paper and string.

Wrapping up a parcel.

Folding paper, folding paper cut to shape.

Formal Activities

1. To teach the child to make independent strong strokes with
   (a) large crayon,
   (b) small crayon.
   (continue to use small crayon once child has co-ordination)
   Take a large sheet of coloured paper and stick on 2 (later 3) squares of white paper. Place this on table in front of child, point to the square and show him how to make a mark in it. Decrease

the size of the square gradually down to about 1" and increase number of squares.

2. Child fills in large square (progressing to circle, triangle etc.,) which is clearly edged by plasticine, thick black line, bright coloured crayon, pencil line. Progress to smaller shapes and put two or more on the same sheet at different angles to encourage movement of crayon at different angles.

3. Using the template for the circle (as used in the informal programme) encourage awareness of the shape by letting the child place his finger inside the template and run it round the edge, then with the chalk in the same way. Then let him hold the template against the blackboard, run the chalk round the inside of the template, move it away and let him see (and feel) the result of his activity. Let him do this lots of times in succession, moving the chalk round in a rhythmic way—he will need a lot of guidance to begin with but as his chalk begins to move more smoothly round the shape, he will gradually be able to take over the task himself. When he can do it easily, remove the template and draw a double thick outline of the shape so that the child is presented with "tramlines" between which he can take his chalk and draw the circle. For the child with very poor sight these outlines can be raised by making a glue line and shaking sand onto it. You can progress from the blackboard to paper and crayon and for the poor sighted child the tramlines can be pricked out. When he copes with the tramlines, make the space between them narrower until it is reduced to a single line which can also be reduced until it is very thin and light and can finally disappear so that the child finds himself managing without any guidelines.

   The same technique can be used to teach a straight line, vertical, horizontal, then combining to form a cross. Follow with the square triangle etc. (see Fig 1) eventually to the letters of the alphabet. (Make sure that the letters are drawn in the correct directions)

4. Teach child to join two dots or crosses which you have marked on a sheet of paper—to begin with these should be about 1" apart and the distance can be gradually increased to about 5". They should be joined horizontally, then vertically and diagonally from both sides, from top to bottom and bottom to top, from left to right and right to left. To make it more interesting you can draw little figures, say a boy and a girl each holding an end of a skipping rope—child has to draw in skipping rope, or a rope from a car to a breakdown lorry, or a string between a hand and some balloons.

5. *Tracking*   Teach child to drive cars along tracks, toy animals or people to walk along roads etc. Graduate the difficulty in two ways:

   (a)   change the road from straight to curved, then to winding.

100

(b) boundaries at first need to be made with bricks or fences, wide apart gradually becoming narrower eventually becoming lines drawn on paper or on blackboard flat on floor, or raised by using string for the child who needs touch clues.

You need to have a definite start and finish i.e. car goes from the house to a garage (drawn or models), animals from a farm to a field, people from home to shop or school etc.

As an additional game child can move a torch beam along the roads or the child with only light/darkness appreciation make his car follow the track of the torch beam along the road.

At a much later stage when the child is beginning to learn the letter shapes, construct plastic railway lines in the letter shapes and let child push the train round them in order to learn the shape and movement involved. Use points to make it easier to show "going back over" as in d and a. Always put ramp to the left and buffers to the right at the end. Progression from this activity is to take a pencil round the track and then to be able to follow the shape without actually touching. This also links with the "tram-line" exercises on the chalkboard mentioned under (3).

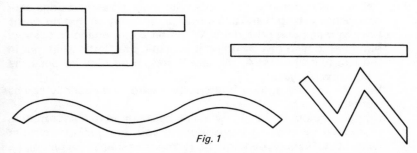

Fig. 1

6. *Pasting*   On to strips of coloured sugar paper (about 6" deep) stick 3" squares of white paper (to identify position for partially sighted child and give raised surface for the child with poor sight). Child is shown how to put a blob of paste on to each square and then to stick a piece of coloured tissue paper in each on top of the paste. When he can do this without help, you can use larger sheets of sugar paper and have more (and smaller) squares (or circles or any other shapes) on which he has to put paste and paper (or scrap material) and in time form patterns. Alternatively you can have one larger shape and stick lots of small pieces of coloured tissue all over it.

7. *Matchstick patterns*   Used matches of the large kind. Stick on to cards in following designs. L △ ▢ N
Child looks at or feels these and, given the appropriate number of

101

matchsticks, copies design.

8. *Counters* Beginning with 3 and working up to 8, stick rows of coloured counters on to cards and draw matching circles underneath on to which child has to place the appropriate counter, always working from left to right. When he can manage rows in this way, give him cards with countersize circles drawn on them in patterns which child covers with counters.

Games similar to those with the counters can also be played with smarties, acorns, buttons and any small objects that could be placed on to the drawn position.

9. *Figure-ground* Follow with finger a line drawn (or raised) on paper (about foolscap size) which say links a man with a dot, a boy with a kite etc. When child can do this, have two such lines which cross each other, at first differing in colour (or texture string, wool stuck over drawn line) and increase in number and vary direction to make more complex. For the partially sighted child you can also do this kind of exercise on the blackboard with chalks, lines, and when these get dense you can trace a line through with a wet cloth and the child has to hurry along this before it dries!

10. *Pegboards* Begin with boards with large holes and pegs several inches in length and allow to play randomly so that he learns how to manipulate the pegs. When he can manage this, show him how to fill a row by doing it yourself, then letting him put in the last two, the last 4, the last 6 and so on until he does the whole row like yours.

Vary the row by putting it down the board or diagonally across from the corners.

Combine colour matching (when he has learned to colour match, of course) by copying the colours in your line, using alternate colours etc. When you know he recognises shapes he can make shapes with the pegs.

For the child with very poor sight you can stick texture on the pegs (you need the large kind for this) and then he can make pegboard work more interesting by matching textures.

Copying patterns actually made by the pegs is followed by making patterns on the pegboard to match designs drawn (or stuck, if texture is being used) on to cards.

At a more advanced stage part lines, or rows of which some holes are not filled, should be given for copying as this helps to draw attention to the spaces—reading and writing depends on observing the position of spaces between words as well as on the words themselves.

11. *Painting* Begin with lots and lots of random painting, bright colours and large sheets of paper (or newspaper) on table, on

floor and on easel.

Finger, foot, comb and finally brush painting.

Thick paint, thin paint, paint mixed with other materials (Polycel, flour and starch paste, washingup liquid,) to give texture.

Paint over whole sheets with one colour.

Paint lines down and across paper.

Paint on paper cut into circles, squares and triangles.

Paint within bounds—inside circle, square, etc.

A very useful piece of apparatus for encouraging child to use paints to copy movement and patterns is a large sheet of strong glass, preferably pivotted at centre and supported in frame (on wheels), together with powder paints, torch and wet cloth.

Child and teacher face each other through the glass. Plane of vision—horizontal or vertical.

Fig. 2

Procedure

(a) Child and teacher can be in a darkened room so that torch light can be better appreciated. One adult shines light on to glass and "draws" a pattern with the light, i.e. circles, lines, patterns. What the torch-holder does, a second adult tries to help child copy with his painted finger, hand or brush. The torchlight can be partly obscured by placing a sheet of paper over the glass (at the torch side). If a record of the child's copy is wanted, then paper can be placed on the child's side.

(b) Adult draws with coloured paint and the child copies the drawing—child preferably using a different colour.

12. *Cutting*

    Stage 1. Large tongs—child uses to pick up small bricks.

           2. Sugar tongs and/or tweezers to pick up corks, beads or smaller things.

           3. Using scissors:

               Cut fringe round outside of firm paper.

               Cut across card between two thick lines $\frac{1}{4}''$ apart gradually decrease thickness of lines and space between.

Cut across single lines, thick at first, decreasing.

Cut through "tunnels" made by sticking long piece of paper on shorter piece.

Cut across diagonally, double lines at first, then single.

Cut round shapes mounted on paper.

Cut round circles, squares etc., between double lines and then along single lines.

Cutting out simple figures.

For the child with poor sight lines can be raised by sticking on string or pricking lines with pin.

Sample Programmes

No. 1

Materials—8 bricks 4 each of two colours or textures.

Activities
(i)   Child has to pile up on top of each other and then knock down (hand-eye co-ordination).
(ii)   Child sorts into two colours (Visual perception).
(iii) Child sets out in pattern of alternate colours (Pre-reading).
(iv) Child takes a brick in each hand and bangs together in imitation of adult.

No. 2

Materials—12 bricks—and a drumstick.

Activities
(i)   Child puts one brick on each of 6 to 8 squares stuck or drawn on sheet of paper (visual/motor).
(ii)   Child copies adult's brick patterns, up or across

1
12
123   (number).

(iii) Child makes bricks into train and/or tunnel, and plays with (imaginative play).
(iv) Set out bricks in row with spaces between to represent rhythm, child bangs with drumstick.

No. 3

Materials—Pegboard and pegs, 12 of each of 3 colours.

Activities
(i)   Puts pegs in board randomly (manual dexterity).

(ii)   Completes a line begun by adult (handeye co-ordination).
(iii) Puts a peg in each corner of board (spatial awareness).
(iv)   Copies a 4-peg square.

No. 4
Materials—6 small bricks 3 of each of two colours
          6 large bricks 3 of each of two colours

Activities
(i)   Sorts for large and small (number).
(ii)   Finds all the bricks of one colour (Visual perception).
(iii) Makes row of alternative sizes.
(iv)   Places large ones on large squares and small ones on small ones
       on small squares drawn on sheet of paper.

PRE-NUMBER PROGRAMMES

Most of us tend to think of number work as counting, adding, subtract-
ing and so on, forgetting that before learning this kind of thing many
pre-number activities will have been part of a child's natural preschool play at home or in nursery school. Awareness of characteristics
such as big and small, long and short, light and heavy, thick and thin;
awareness of time in terms of first and last, before, after, next; of quantity in terms of same, more, less, enough, too many, one, two, three
etc; of seriation, that is ordering things by relationships, big, bigger,
biggest, first, second, third etc., all this is pre-number and is usually
within the daily experience of a young child. It has been made meaningful to him by feeling, seeing and manipulating and by hearing us
give the appropriate names.

It is true that many young children learn to count by rote, but learning
to use number names meaningfully comes only slowly alongside the
above—a child of 3 years can usually give you one thing or two things
if asked, but will still give you two things or more than two things if you
ask for three—and using number symbols, learning to measure by
counting and describing in numerical terms comes much later. Progress in number work will be very slow for most deaf/blind children
and a realistic aim is for them ultimately to know enough to see them
through their daily living—to be able to go shopping, tell the time, pay
fares on transport, be able to recognise bus and house numbers. A
good many will not reach this stage, but we must take them through
the sequence as far as we can.

Some of the play materials in the final phase of the Early Play Experiences have had a number element—playing peep-boo (one or
nothing), nesting toys, sand and water. We shall continue to use play

materials together with some specific but easily obtained items, but we will use them in such a way that the child's attention is drawn to the concepts that are learned from pre-number activities. In the pre-school period the deaf/blind child's programme should consist of (1) sorting, (2) seriating and (3) matching, each section having its own progressive sequence.

1. Sorting

All number is concerned with groups. Sorting is the most simple way of grouping—"the same" and "not the same", all the red ones; the red ones and the blue ones; and so on.

Informal

Spoons and forks.
Socks and shoes.
Vests and pants.
Buttons (colour and shape).
Conkers in and out of skins.
Cardboard boxes and tins.
Round biscuits and square biscuits.

Formal

Sorting objects—i.e. toys cars and bricks; model animals—big contrast (ducks and horses).
Sorting shapes—balls and cubes (one colour); round and square (triangles).
Sorting texture—i.e. velvet and sandpaper etc stuck on toilet roll centres.
Sorting colour—objects i.e. red balls and blue balls etc; cardboard squares with coloured sticky paper.
Sorting colour/shape—red and blue squares with red and blue circles, to be sorted into all the circles or all the red things.
Texture/shape—silk covered squares and triangles with rough covered squares and triangles to be sorted into all the rough ones or all the squares.
Length—rods, straws etc—find all the long ones; all the short ones.
These examples use only two contrasting items, as the child becomes proficient with two, sorting out three sets of things, then four and so on can be introduced under the first four headings.

Procedure

It is best to have the material to be sorted in a tray and to sort into trays which when training is begun can provide a clue to the task by being lined with the appropriate colour, texture or marked with the appropriate shape. The lids of shoe boxes make good trays or you can use the shallow trays in which some foods are sold.

The child with useful sight should begin with objects and then colour, the child with poor sight objects and then texture. Once they understand the task, you can proceed through the sequence. Show the child what you want him to do by doing it yourself, then take his hand, draw attention to the relevant characteristics by pointing or touch, then help him by holding his hand and guiding the sorting into the right trays.

1a. Sorting for Size

Informal

Awareness of size in comparison to himself.
> Hands, feet etc—mummy's are big, his are small.
> Things for crawling through—hoops, tyres, tunnels etc.
> Boxes to climb in and out.
> Dressing up—clothes too big and too small.

Awareness of size variation of similar objects.
> Ball play of various kinds using very big balls and small ones from giant balls to roll over to pingpong balls to blow along.
> Play with sets of dolls, shells, pencils etc of different sizes.
> The three bears—with appropriate chair, bowls, beds etc.
> Jokes—child is given tablespoon to eat egg or stir tea, or teaspoon to serve himself potato etc, giant plastic combs such as you can get at seaside shops or very tiny dolls comb to do his own hair; daddy's shoe instead of his own and so on.
> Oblong piece of wood with 3 or 4 bolts through it—child given variety of nuts to screw on some too small, some too big.

Formal

Materials   1 dozen each big and small spoons, combs, balls, toy cars, dolls, shoes, wooden blocks

Procedure   The sorting should be done into a big box and a small box.

Language   Where there is a reasonable sight use gestures that indicate big and small together with the appropriate adjective i.e. *big* spoon, *small* spoon, in the *big* box, the *small* box etc. If signs are used sign big or small and holding the child's hands in yours make the gestures for big and small with him. Encourage him to feel the difference in size.

Let him explore the boxes before beginning with the material.

1. One type of material only i.e. the big and small spoons all mixed together. Show the child that you want the big ones to go into the big box and the small ones in the small box, then help him do it using appropriate language (as above). When he begins to do it for himself always put a sample one in the appropriate box for him

107

—eventually when he gets proficient he will not need this aid.

Using the same technique work through the simple to the complex as follows:

2. Work through each set of objects individually.
3. Mix together two half-sets of big and small items, i.e. 6 big and small spoons with 6 big and small spoons.
4. Mix together three half-sets of big and small items.
5. Mix together an assortment of big and small items from all the sets. The materials allow for a variety of combinations.

Make sure you always use the same adjectives i.e. use big and small NOT large and small or big or little—in fact it does not matter which two you use so long as you stick to those two, otherwise the child will become very confused.

When you feel the concept of big and small is understood and the child understands the word or sign, he will enjoy finding you big ones and small ones from a big bag by feeling or fetching you the appropriate one from a number placed on a table or tray a little way away from where you are playing.

To begin with the size difference wants to be extreme, but once the idea is understood, you can make the difference less and less. Quisenaire rods are useful for this, but it is quite an advanced stage.

1b. Sorting for Long and Short; Thick and Thin; Light and Heavy

Informal

Long and short—skirts, trousers and sleeves too long or short, taking long and short steps, fitting things into boxes, packets of biscuits into short box, etc.

Thick and thin—slices of bread, posting box with thick and thin openings for thick and thin bricks, crayoning on thin paper and card.

Weight—trying to lift things that are too heavy, playing with balloon/weighted ball, filling buckets with a lot or a little sand and carrying about, etc. Play with simple balance scales.

Formal

Materials   Long and short—Pieces of string, card, bricks, straws.

Thick and thin—Circular pieces of wood, polystyrene tile, or any material which can be very obviously thick and thin. Use one material at a time making sure that only the thickness varies not the texture or colour.

Light and heavy—Sealed tins, bags or boxes containing sand, flour, rice or no sand, flour, rice.

Procedure   For long and short and for thick and thin use the same sorting procedure as for big and small, going from the simple to the complex, using appropriate language.

Freeplay with the light and heavy material is probably sufficient at this stage.
Make the differences extreme.

2. Seriating
Sorting for size as under (1a) is preliminary to seriation. Only when the contrast between big and small is understood can you introduce an intermediate "middle" which is where this skill begins. The idea of size order must be understood before you can learn to sequence the categories under (1b).

Informal
Play with different sizes of tins, cartons, bricks of same shape and colour, but different sizes, grading toys such as graded inset boards, rings on sticks, people/animal rings on sticks, inset cylinders etc.

Formal
Using clay, plasticine, playdoh, or dough:
1. Child is shown how to roll "sausages" and "balls" and then makes a big one for Daddy, a small one for himself and a middle one for Mummy.
2. Have three different sized dolls and suitably **sized** clothes for them, also other items which can be played with to match the dolls, i.e. three cups, spoons, balls and so on.
3. Sets of sticks, pencils, spoons, bricks or any toy that child enjoys in varying size and show child how to line up in order from small to large in left to right direction. Square bricks built up to make stairs.
4. Get child to estimate size for himself:
   (a) Given a lump of plasticine and a big brick and a small brick, make a big ball to put on the big brick and a small ball to put on the small brick.
   (b) Given a lump of plasticine and a series of graded bricks, make graded balls to go with the bricks.

3. Matching for Number
All experience of "sameness" is relative to this skill as are the exercises in matching which have been suggested under the heading "pre-reading", but we now need to match in a one-to-one relationship.

Informal
Finger and toe games—"This little pig went to market", "Two little dicky birds"—where the action denotes the number aspect. Matching handclaps (adults hands round child makes the pattern, when adult stops child copies). Counting on to the fingers to match going up

stairs, buttons on clothes, biscuits on to plate for tea, wheels on toy car, sharing out sweets etc—one for you, one for me and so on.

Formal

1. A number of small containers (e.g. eggcups) into each of which child puts one thing, plastic mugs into each of which child puts two spoons and so on.
2. Child copies tower of 2 bricks, 3 bricks, 4 and then 5.
3. Puts counters on circles drawn on card e.g.

   O   O
   O   O   O

   For the child with poor sight these circles can be of a raised surface—sandpaper etc.
4. Cards with large printed or raised dot patterns up to 5, for sorting —or domino bricks.
5. Matching number on abacus or pegboard i.e. adult puts in three pegs on one side of peg board, child puts in matching number on the other side.
6. Adult puts 2 cars on table, child matches by putting two underneath. Any small toys can be used for this kind of game. Increase up to 5 gradually.
7. Play with sand and water filling large containers from small ones (jugfuls, spoonfuls, cupfuls). Adult makes rows of different number of sandpies—child makes matching row.

CHAPTER 12
SCHOOL YEARS AND AFTER

It is not the purpose of this book to give advice for the school years. In these years co-operation between home and school should determine the day to day and year by year programming. Whatever school programme your child enters he will be helped to continue along the educational pathway according to his ability. At the time of writing deaf /blind children find their way into a variety of schools or units, some specially catering for the deaf/blind, some for the deaf, for the blind or for the partially sighted, or day special schools and hospital schools which take multiply handicapped children. It is natural that the child with the greater intellectual ability should attend the school catering for children of that level—often a sore point with parents who feel if only their child could go to such a school, miracles would happen. There is good reason to feel like this if such a school is the only one to meet all demands, but nowadays with a greater understanding of the educational needs of deaf/blind children, they can be catered for adequately at different levels in different schools. Also there should now be more opportunity for a deaf/blind child to move to a school with a more academic bias if he shows himself more able than at first believed. Equally so if the pressures of a school are too much for a deaf /blind child at any stage he should be able to move to a school where the training proceeds at a more suitable pace. We should not regard such moves, if they occur, as "up" or "down", but as the best way of meeting the particular needs of the individual child.

Some of the schools taking deaf/blind pupils are boarding schools. Unless these are weekly boarding schools, it is extremely difficult to keep the close contact between home and school which provides for the all important continuity of handling, and communication techniques. With the less able deaf/blind child if he is away for the whole of a term, or even a half-term, homecoming can be like facing a new set of people in a new environment and it can take the whole of a long summer for parents to really get to know their child again. Except for special cases, a day school is best for the child, and, in the long, run, for the parents.

If you have been able to work through some or all of the programmes in this book on your own, with help or in conjuction with the teacher if your child attends preschool group, starting school should not present too many problems. For the child it will represent continuity of activity (and possibly teacher) and familiarity with materials and routines will help him to settle. For you the parent it will represent a change in role, no longer iniating the teaching programme, but complementing the work of the teacher. The importance of close contact with the school cannot be over-emphasised and if must be a genuine two-way process. You must keep aware of what your child is learning, so that you follow the same pattern of communication, occupation and social routines. Unless everybody concerned with the child during his waking hours deals with him in the same way all through these waking hours, he will not benefit to the full.

Employment

Schooldays officially end somewhere between 16 and 17 years although the majority of deaf/blind children will probably not have reached the limits of their educational potential. We parents therefore have to resume the role of teacher when our child finishes school and be concerned not so much with teaching new skills (except for leisure occupations) as increasing in depth and breadth those which the child enjoys. Every effort must be made to increase communication skills and the method used during schooldays kept up within the circle of the young persons family and friends. Special facilities for further education for the handicapped are few, but are on the increase and likely in the future to include vocational training schemes and opportunities for educational, social and emotional growth. There is also a great need for centres where the transition from school to employment (whether this is open or sheltered) can be bridged and the young deaf /blind person can experience a taste of independence.

The following choice of employment and occupation exists today:

Employment in open industry.
Factories such as Remploy.
Sheltered workshops.
Senior Training Centres.
Work to be done at home.
Hospital training centres.

Only a few have so far managed to get jobs in open industry, a few more are working in sheltered workshops and by far the largest group are in Senior or Hospital Training Centres. With earlier and better educational prospects, there should gradually be less in the last group and more in the sheltered workshops. Occasionally sheltered workshops and Senior Training Centres have their own hostels and with the present trend towards more community living for the handicapped, it is hoped that the idea of small groups living as a family sharing a house with houseparents will also be possible for the deaf/blind in due course of time.

However many deaf/blind young people do have to live at home after schooldays and having an adult handicapped son or daughter in the home becomes a great problem as parents grow older. Although we may want to care for them ourselves as long as possible, it is in the long term better for them to have a life-style of their own (even if this is no more than hospital care) but keeping close contact always with their families. It is amazing how, despite lack of intellectual development, our young deaf/blind people grow up and mature. You cannot expect those with severe limitations to the sight and hearing to accept responsibility but they do come to terms with life as they find it and this, after a childhood of ups and downs, struggles and strains, is very rewarding to parents.

Some kind of daily routine which includes a period of regular occupation whatever its level, is absolutely necessary for every handicapped young person or adult. An aimless irregular daily existence can often lead to a gradual withdrawal, loss of energy and emotional problems. Even our most handicapped deaf/blind have a need for regular work and leisure periods as do all of us. A lot of thought is now being given to discarding the idea that handicapped people only need care and instead to provide greater opportunity for them to lead a more full and satisfying life. It is possible that in the next decade we shall see many improvements. Almost every group of handicapped young people have employment and occupation difficulties—if your son or daughter is the only deaf/blind one for miles around and there seems to be absolutely nothing available through official sources it is worth contacting parents of young folk with other handicaps and seeing what can be done in co-operation with them.

Social Activities

Where it has been within the capabilities of the deaf/blind child, his school will have provided opportunity for extending the mobility training beyond the confines of the school to visiting local shops, using public transport and so on. This must be kept up when the child leaves school—it may mean the careful learning about an area with which he is not familiar any longer, or never has been, if he is at boarding school. If he has learned to get around a bit by himself in one place he can do it in another and we must not let him lose a skill which is so vital to independence. There are specially trained Mobility officers with whom you can get in touch through the Director of Social Services in your Local Authority to help you to do this.

Playing active games competitively is generally denied the deaf/blind, but it does depend on the amount of residual sight—I know of two who play tennis. But horse riding, swimming and walking are activities very much enjoyed by them and there are few who do not also enjoy a ride in a car or a train. Many show a liking for jigsaws and some learn to play ludo, dominoes, card and dice games. The Royal National Institute for the Blind provides a variety of games of this sort where the parts are identified by braille dots or some kind of tactile clue. Chess is a game which has been played at Championship level by at least one deaf/blind boy.

Many parents in the past have complained of the lack of social facilities for the deaf/blind. They are generally too few in number for anything special to be organised locally and unfortunately they do not seem to get on too well in adult blind or deaf groups. The Deaf/Blind Helpers League has local clubs which are run by the deaf/blind themselves and are generally made up of the older people who have lost their sight and hearing later in life—but the young deaf/blind are always made very welcome. Senior Training Centres sometimes also have their own Social Clubs and there are the Gateway Clubs for the Mentally Handicapped about which your local branch of the National Society for Mentally Handicapped Children will be able to advise you. Even if participation is not possible, going out and being in a place which is different and has another atmosphere, is good for our youngsters as for any other.

Holidays

When the child is young it is quite a good idea to let him go to a short-stay holiday home whilst you and the rest of the family have a holiday on your own. Local Authorities and Regional Hospital Boards are empowered to provide these facilities and you enquire about them at your local Town Hall. A list of private places can be obtained from the National Deaf/Blind and Rubella Children's Association. If you wish to take your child on holiday with you, the above Association (and many others) have caravans at seaside resorts for which only a nominal charge is made and which are kept for the use only of families with handicapped children. A holiday is necessary for everybody at some time during the year and having the care of a handicapped child makes this even more necessary for his family. If you like holidays abroad there is no reason why you should not take your child with you, but do check with the relevant Embassy or High Commissioner to make certain that his entry to the country to which you are going is permitted.

Sources of advice and assistance

Parents very often do not seek help and advice that they really need and could have because they do not know where to go for it. With the greater understanding of the handicapped child has grown a greater understanding of the stresses his care lays upon his family and the modern trend is to help the child by helping his family.

A great many booklets and leaflets are issued by Government departments and Local Authorities giving detailed information about services, financial help etc., (which can, of course, differ from area to area) so the following is no more than a broad guide to where to start.

APPENDIX

Welfare

National Health Service (Government Department)
FREE PRESCRIPTIONS   All children under 15
   If your child is over 15 and receiving Supplementary Benefit.
DENTAL TREATMENT AND GLASSES   Anyone receiving Supplementary Benefit and free prescriptions is automatically entitled to an additional payment to meet the cost of dental treatment and glasses.
HEARING AIDS   are available free on permanent loan when prescribed. Aids are serviced, maintained and supplied with batteries without charge.
NO CHARGE FOR   Hospital services, Home visit of consultant if arranged by your family Doctor.
More detailed information to be found in Booklets E.C.91, P.C.11 and E.C.95.

Local Authority Social & Health Service
Contact the Director of Social Services for:
VISIT FROM SOCIAL WORKER   To give support, advice and personal help whenever difficulties arise. A source of information on what statutory and voluntary services are available in your area.
SPECIALIST SOCIAL WORKERS *For the blind*—advice to parents, on mobility, rehabilitation; residential, convalescent and holiday accommodation; instructions on handicrafts and help in learning Braille and moon type.
   For the deaf—advice to parents; interpreters, lipreading classes.
DAY NURSERY OR PLAY GROUP PROVISION   For handicapped children under school age.

DAY CENTRES   For light industry or contract work (regular or in preparation for employment). For social activities and handicrafts. (Transport to and from these centres is often provided.)

INFORMATION RE: Organisations able to help in way of specific jobs i.e. shopping, baby-minding, etc.
British Talking Book for the Blind Service.
Free loan of radio for Registered Blind people. Availability of large type books for the partially sighted at your local public library.

Contact your County Medical Officer for:

HEALTH VISITOR   Advice on the health of your child.

NURSE   If the home nursing of a handicapped child or person is necessary.

CHILD HEALTH CLINIC   Special health needs, examinations and screening tests.

LAUNDRY SERVICE   To help in households where there is a handicapped person. Incontinence pads are supplied in some areas.

CHIROPODY   At local clinic.

RESIDENTIAL HOMES   For temporary or permanent residence of handicapped persons (charges according to ability to pay).

Financial Assistance

Department of Health & Social Security (Government Department)
Contact your local Social Security Office re:

SUPPLEMENTARY BENEFITS   If you are 16 and over and not in fulltime work. The amount you receive is the difference between your requirements for everyday living expenses (laid down by Parliament) and any income you may have. There are special rates for registered blind persons.

ATTENDANCE ALLOWANCE   This allowance is for children over 2 and adults over 16 who are severely physically or mentally disabled, or who need a lot of looking after. A higher rate is available for those who need looking after both day and night; a lower rate is available for those needing attendance by day or night. This allowance is tax free.

FREE WELFARE MILK   If your child is between 5 and 16 and is not attending an educational establishment. (This concession is available to parents during the time children in hospital are home on holiday) (Leaflet No.W.11).

THE FAMILY FUND   This is a fund established by the Government to help the parents of very severely handicapped children in the United Kingdom which is designed specifically to relieve stress in families by complementing the provision of services and cash benefits from both statutory and voluntary sources. The Handicap must be congenital (or manifest within 28 days of birth) and it is ap-

116

plicable to parents of the children at birth and up to the age of 16. It is administered on behalf of the Government by the Joseph Rowntree Memorial Trust (Beverley House, Shipton Road, York, YO3 6RB) to whom parents should apply for a form (or it can be obtained from your Social Worker). Grants have been made to provide the following kind of help and equipment:

Car grants, driving lessons, self-hire charges, taxi fares and other travelling expenses.

Caravans, holidays, electric wheel chairs, washing machines, driers, deep freezers, sewing machines, record players, clothing and bedding.

Housing loans and adaptation grants, central heating, cookers, special bathing and toiletting equipment. Home help.

Educational equipment, playpool, toys etc.

Contact your Local Authority Social and Health Services Dept., for financial aids as follows:

SPECIAL CONCESSIONS FOR REGISTERED BLIND PEOPLE

Special Income Tax allowance (apply local Inspector of Taxes).

T.V. licence at reduced cost (apply P.O.)

Free postage on items sent as "articles for the blind"

Travel Concessions—British Rail, London Transport, local bus undertakings and B.E.A. internal flights in connection with blind person's guide.

HOME HELP   In cases of special need.

HOUSING   Grants towards adaptations which make it easier for a handicapped person to look after himself or for others to look after him. Grants towards bringing a house up to recognised standard (toilet and bathroom improvements) if this is in the interests of the handicapped person.

(Apply Housing Department).

TELEPHONES   In cases of real need, help with telephones may be provided—but not the cost of calls.

Education (local authority) (Contact Chief Education Officer)

Your local Education Department will arrange a medical examination for any child who may be handicapped. Referral may be via your family doctor, a pediatrician or following assessment at a special centre. Depending on the availability of such facilities in your area, your child is entitled to special educational treatment according to his needs from the age of 2 years.

NURSERY SCHOOL   Attached to a normal school or a special school.

SPECIAL UNIT   Attached to normal school (day or residential).

SPECIAL SCHOOL   Dealing with specific handicaps i.e. for the deaf, blind, partially sighted, multiply handicapped. (day and residential).

DAY SPECIAL SCHOOL   Catering for the multiply handicapped.

HOME TEACHER   If child cannot attend any of the above.

FURTHER EDUCATION   A few Local Authorities run special Courses for the handicapped or have arrangements with nearby colleges to help handicapped students wishing to take additional courses. They will also provide special help—braille writing machines, possums, or interpreters for the deaf where necessary.

Employment

Department of Employment (Government Department)

Special Services for the Handicapped.

A. Contact the Disablement Resettlement Officer (D.R.O.) at your local Employment Exchange for advice on:

   Disabled Persons Register This is for severely handicapped people over 18—entitles you to consideration for special training schemes which might be available in your area, certain sheltered employment and guidance in connection with employers who have a statutory obligation to employ a certain quota of registered disabled persons.

   Information about courses for training or rehabilitation if you need training for a change of job.

B. Contact the Blind Persons Resettlement Officer for special facilities etc., for registered blind people.

Youth Employment Service (local authority)

A handicapped person *under* the age of 18 and able to work, should contact the Careers Officer of this Service for advice and help in finding a suitable job.

All the special services as above apply to England and Wales. Information for the handicapped in Scotland can be found in the following booklets: "A Guide to Welfare Benefits and Citizens' Rights": Obtain from Social Work Department, 14, Castle Terrace, Edinburgh EH. 2EF "Help for Handicapped People in Scotland". Prepared by Scottish Office, Department of Health and Social Security and the Department of Employment. Obtain from Social Work Services Group, York Buildings, Queen St., Edinburgh EH. 21HY

Specialised Further Education/Training Establishments

The following provide for the visually handicapped:

College for Shorthand Typists and Telephonists, London W.2. (R.N.I.B.)

   Twenty-eight people of either sex and aged 16 plus pursue courses in telephone, audio-typing and shorthand and typing. These courses last for two, eight and 12 months respectively.

Heathersett, Reigate, Surrey. (R.N.I.B.).

   Forty-two adolescents attend assessment and vocational guid-

118

ance courses which last on average three or four terms.

Queen Alexandra College, Harborne, Birmingham (Birmingham R.I.B.)

Assessment and vocational guidance courses for 45 young people. These courses last for two to four terms. There is also an engineering course which lasts approximately 18 months.

Royal Normal College for the Blind, Rowton Castle, Shrewsbury.

Offers further education and vocational training courses for 140 students of either sex aged 16 plus. Courses last for between two and four years.

School of Physiotherapy, London W.1. (R.N.I.B.)

Provides fully recognised training in physiotherapy leading to the professional qualification of the Chartered Society of Physiotherapists, for 48 visually handicapped young people. The course lasts 3 years.

Voluntary Organisations

National Deaf/Blind & Rubella Association, Sec. Mrs. P. Hills, 61, Senneleys Park Road, Northfields, Birmingham 31.

Concerned with the welfare of deaf/blind children. Guidance for their parents, grants for toys, carrying and mobility equipment, travelling, holiday caravans, meetings for parents, 5-yearly conferences, regular Newsletter.

Royal National Institute for the Deaf. The General Secretary, 105, Gower Street, London W.C.1.

Deaf children and adults including those with additional handicaps. Facilities include a school for maladjusted deaf children, hearing aid advice service, residential homes which take deaf/blind adults, clubs, classes, monthly journal, library, etc.

Royal National Institute for the Blind, 224, Great Portland Street, London W.1.

Blind and deaf/blind children and adults. All services including Sunshine Homes for the young blind child, schools for the blind some specially geared to the needs of the deaf/blind or multiply handicapped blind child. Library of books in braille or moon print —free loan, students' braille and tape library. A wide range of special aids and appliances available at reduced prices for blind people.

The National Society for Mentally Handicapped Children, 86, Newman Street, London W1P 4AR.

Many parents of the more severely handicapped deaf/blind children find it useful to belong to this Association and to attend their meetings for parents. Often there are too few deaf/blind children in an area to arrange special meetings locally for their parents and the

N.S.M.H.C. has many local branches which organise not only activities for parents, but also for the children and young folk.

They also have a Trusteeship Scheme through which you can provide for your child's interests when you are no longer there to do this for yourself. To enter this scheme members must either provide (now or in your will) the sum of five hundred pounds or effect a Life Assurance Policy for this sum (assigning the policy to the Society). It provides for a Welfare Visitor to supervise the child's wellbeing for the rest of his life after your decease to:

1. Visit the child regularly, become his friend, take him out and remember birthdays and Christmas.
2. Become conversant with the child's background and special needs and ensure that all that ought to be done is carried out efficiently.
3. To keep contact with Local Authorities, hospitals and other bodies responsible for the care of the child and take action, with the support of the N.S.M.H.C. if necessary, in the event of special difficulties.

Information on this scheme can be obtained from:

The Secretary, The Board of Management, Trusteeship Scheme, 86, Newman Street, London W.1.

BOOK LIST

Books, Reports etc.

1. *About the Deaf/Blind*

"Reports on the First, Second and Third Conferences on Children with a combined Visual & Auditory Handicap held 1961, 1966 and 1971" Peggy Freeman (Ed.). (National Association for Deaf/Blind & Rubella Children).

Educational Beginnings with Deaf/Blind Children, Nan Robbins (Perkins School for the Blind, Boston, U.S.A. 1960).

Speech Beginnings for the Deaf/Blind Child, Nan Robbins (Perkins School for the Blind, Boston, U.S.A. 1963).

Auditory Training in the Perkins Deaf/Blind Department, Nan Robbins (Perkins School for the Blind, Boston, U.S.A. 1964).

The Deaf/Blind "Rubella" Child, Nan Robbins & G. Stenquist (Perkins School for the Blind, Boston, U.S.A. 1967).

Body Image of the Deaf/Blind Rubella Child, Virginia Guldager (Perkins School for the Blind, Boston, U.S.A.).

"The Preschool deaf/blind child" "Toilet Habits". (Booklets by the American Foundation for the Blind, New York. 10011).

The Story of my Life, Helen Keller (Doubleday & Co. New York, 1903).

Teacher, Helen Keller (Doubleday & Co. New York, 1955).

Child of the Silent Night, Edith Hunter (Houghton Mifflin, 1963).

Life at My Fingertips, Robert J. Smithdas (Doubleday & Co. New York).

"International Conferences on the Education of Deaf/Blind Children"

The Teaching of deaf/blind children (England 1st 1962); The Teaching of deaf/blind children (Denmark 2nd 1965); Modern Approaches to the Diagnosis and Instruction of Multi-Handicapped Children (Holland, 3rd 1968); Serving Deaf/Blind Children (Boston, U.S.A. 4th 1971).

1st and 2nd can be obtained from Royal National Institute for the Blind, 3rd from the Rotterdam University Press and the 4th from Perkins School for the Blind.

2. *Books about Child Development and Handicaps in general*

The First 5 Years of Life, Arnold Gesel (Methuen & Co. Ltd).

The Abilities of Babies, R. Griffiths (University of London Press).

The Development of the Infant & Young Child, Illingworth (Pub. Livingstone).

The Young Aphasic Child, H. Barry (Alexander Graham Bell).

The Slow Learner in the Classroom, N. C. Kephart (Merrill Publishing Co).

Motoric Aids to Perceptual Training Chaney & Kephart (Merrill Publishing Co.).

Frostig Program for the Development of Visual Perception, M. Frostig (Follett Publishing Co.).

Reading and Remedial Reading, A. E. Tansley (Routledge & Kegan Paul).

Teach Your Baby to Read, Glenn Doman (Jonathan Cape).

Reading & Writing Before School, F. Hughes (Jonathan Cape).

3. *Books and articles of interest to teachers*

Behaviour Modification Programs for Deaf/Blind Children, (Pinecrest State School, Pineville, Louisiana, U.S.A.).

"A Close Look at . . ." (San Gabriel Valley School, Azusa, Calif. U.S.A.).

The Deaf/Blind Child: Diagnosis and Training, H. R. Myklebust (Perkins School for the Blind, Boston, U.S.A.).

Leaves in an Eastern Wind, (IV), H. G. Williams, (Work with deaf/blind children in Russia) 1963.61.183–198 Teacher of the Deaf.

"Visual Impairment Among Deaf Children—frequency and educational consequences", R.G. Suchman. (*Volta Review* 1968 *70* (1)).

121

"The First Steps of deaf/blind children towards language", J. Van Dijk. (*International Journal of the Education of the Blind* 1966.5.).

"The Deaf-Blind Person: a review of the literature", P. J. Salmon and H. Rusalem (*In Blindness A WWB Annual,* 1966.

A Reading Guide to assist research workers in reviewing materials on the problems of the Deaf/Blind Multi-handicapped child prepared by W. S. Curtis and E. T. Dondon, Directors of the Multiple Disabilities Project at the Syracuse University, Syracuse, New York.

Suppliers of Equipment

The following firms produce equipment suitable for deaf/blind children and will send their catalogues on request:

E. J. Arnold & Son Ltd., Butterley Street, Leeds 10

James Galt & Co Ltd., Brookfield Road, Cheadle, Cheshire

E. S. A. Ltd., Pinnacles, Harlow, Essex

Reeves & Son Ltd., Lincoln Road, Enfield, Middlesex ("Early Learning")

Taskmaster Ltd., Morris Road, Clarendon Park, Leicester (DLM Developmental Learning Materials 74)

Disabled Living Foundation., 346 Kensington High Street, London W14 8NS (List of publications concerning clothing, footwear, fastening etc for the handicapped child)

Paul & Marjorie Abbatt Ltd., 94 Wimpole Street, London, W 1. ("Development Toys"—in conjunction with book by M & F Morgenstern "Practical Training for the Severely Handicapped Child"—W Heinemann Medical Books Ltd.

INDEX